Masters of Media

Masters of Media

Controversies & Solutions
Volume 1

Victor C. Strasburger, Editor

ROWMAN & LITTLEFIELD
Lanham • Boulder • New York • London

Published by Rowman & Littlefield
A wholly owned subsidiary of The Rowman & Littlefield Publishing Group, Inc.
4501 Forbes Boulevard, Suite 200, Lanham, Maryland 20706
www.rowman.com

Unit A, Whitacre Mews, 26-34 Stannary Street, London SE11 4AB

British Library Cataloguing in Publication Information Available

Library of Congress Cataloging-in-Publication Data

Names: Strasburger, Victor C., 1949- editor.
Title: Masters of media : controversies and solutions / Victor C. Strasburger.
Description: Lanham : Rowman & Littlefield Publishers, 2021. | Includes
    bibliographical references. | Summary: "This book deals with some of the most
    contentious media issues today-media violence, violent video games,
    cyberbullying, sexting, gaming addiction, fake news, and use of media
    in the classroom"— Provided by publisher.
Identifiers: LCCN 2021006299 (print) | LCCN 2021006300 (ebook) |
    ISBN 9781475855210 (v. 1 ; cloth) | ISBN 9781475855227 (v. 1 ; paperback) |
    ISBN 9781475855234 (v. 1 ; epub)
Subjects: LCSH: Mass media and youth. | Violence in mass media. | Cyberbullying. |
    Aggressiveness. | Fake news.
Classification: LCC HQ784.M3 M373 2021 (print) | LCC HQ784.M3 (ebook) |
    DDC 302.23083—dc23
LC record available at https://lccn.loc.gov/2021006299
LC ebook record available at https://lccn.loc.gov/2021006300

~

Contents

~

Preface

Victor C. Strasburger

The way adolescents of today learn, play, and interact has changed more in the past 15 years than in the previous 570 since Gutenberg's popularization of the printing press.

Jay N. Giedd, M.D., (2012)

We put our kids through fifteen years of quick-cut advertising, passive television watching, and sadistic video games, and we expect to see emerge a new generation of calm, compassionate, and engaged human beings?

Sidney Poitier, *The Measure of a Man* (2007)

I doubt I would be here [in the White House] if it weren't for social media, to be honest with you . . . When somebody says something about me, I am able to go bing, bing, bing and I take care of it.

President Donald Trump, quoted by Reuters, October 22, 2017

Media have immense power over children and adolescents—now having become almost as important as the air that they breathe. And the media landscape is changing so rapidly that parents, teachers, administrators, and government officials simply can't keep up. But wait—help is on the way! I hope that this slim volume will aid parents and teachers and others in illuminating the answers to common media controversies and concerns.

It is a truth universally accepted that new media have always come under increased scrutiny (and deservedly so)—witness the following quote from the 1790 book, *Memoirs of the Bloomsgrove Family* by the Reverend Enos Hitchcock:

> The free access which many young people have to romances, novels, and plays has poisoned the mind and corrupted the morals of many a promising youth; and prevented others from improving their minds in useful knowledge. Parents take care to feed their children with wholesome diet; and yet how unconcerned about the provision for the mind, whether they are furnished with salutary food, or with trash, chaff, or poison?

When they first appeared, telephones were feared because people might make secret plans. Dime store novels, comic books, TV, video games, the Internet, now social networking and soon virtual reality—all have elicited significant initial concern and fear. Yet that doesn't mean that scrutiny isn't needed and deserved as each new medium appears.

Pediatricians have been concerned about media effects since the early 1980s—more than 35 years ago (American Academy of Pediatrics, 1984)—and have accepted the fact that media can affect virtually every concern that parents and teachers have about children and adolescents, from aggressive behavior to early sexual intercourse, drug use, eating disorders, early childhood learning, even ADHD (Strasburger, 2020). That said, there can be tremendous variation in how susceptible children and adolescents individually are, even within the same family or classroom; and media can often be powerfully prosocial as well as potentially harmful.

This is the first of several Masters of Media volumes that will attempt to sort out the basic facts—not the "fake news"—behind many of the media stories and reports you've probably heard and possibly worried about. Upcoming will be volumes that focus in detail on social media, health effects, and learning; but many of those topics will be discussed in this issue as well – media violence, video games, gaming addiction, social networking, "fake news," teaching media literacy, cyberbullying, and sexting.

I am extremely grateful to the very accomplished and well-known authors for contributing to this issue.

Vic Strasburger, M.D.
Distinguished Professor of Pediatrics *Emeritus*
University of New Mexico School of Medicine
Albuquerque, NM USA

References

American Academy of Pediatrics, Task Force on Children and Television. (1984). *Children, Adolescents and Television*. Elk Grove Village, IL: AAP.

Giedd, J. N. (2012). The digital revolution and adolescent brain evolution. *Journal of Adolescent Health*, 51(2), 101–105.

Poitier, S. (2007). *The Measure of a Man*. New York: HarperCollins.

Strasburger, V. C. (2020). *The Death of Childhood: Reinventing the Joy of Growing Up*. Cambridge, UK: Cambridge Scholars Press.

CHAPTER 1

~

Introduction

Children, Adolescents, and the Media: Is There a Problem?

Victor C. Strasburger

"We put our kids through fifteen years of quick-cut advertising, passive television watching, and sadistic video games, and we expect to see emerge a new generation of calm, compassionate, and engaged human beings?"—Sidney Poitier, *The Measure of a Man* (2007)

"We live in an age of visual overstimulation. Between the pernicious screen, whether television or motion pictures or computers, and all of their fallouts like BlackBerrys and that sort of stuff – they destroy the ability to read well."—Literary scholar Harold Bloom, quoted in *Time* magazine, May 11, 2015

"Whether we gain or not by this habit of profuse communication it is not for us to say." —Virginia Woolf, *Jacob's Room*, 1922

"I doubt I would be here [in the White House] if it weren't for social media, to be honest with you . . . When somebody says something about me, I am able to go bing, bing, bing and I take care of it."—President Donald Trump, quoted by Reuters, October 22, 2017

Introduction

It is a truth universally acknowledged that every generation thinks the next generations are going to hell in a handbasket. Concerns about media certainly fit into that category. Consider this accusation by the Reverend Enos Hitchcock in a book entitled, *Memoirs of the Bloomsgrove Family:*

> The free access which many young people have to romances, novels, and plays has poisoned the mind and corrupted the morals of many a promising youth; and prevented others from improving their minds in useful knowledge. Parents take care to feed their children with wholesome diet; and yet how unconcerned about the provision for the mind, whether they are furnished with salutary food, or with trash, chaff, or poison?

Although it could conceivably have been written in the new millennium, it was actually written in 1790. The good Reverend was concerned about dime store novels.

The appearance of comic books drew a similar reaction: In a 1948 editorial, the *Christian Science Monitor* attributed the rise in juvenile crime to the "cheap and lurid sensationalism" of comic books. Soon after, Senator Estes Kefauver held hearings in the US Senate about whether media violence on TV was contributing to juvenile delinquency.

Much more recently, Nicholas Kardars (author of *Glow Kids: How Screen Addiction Is Hijacking Our Kids*) received a huge amount of publicity when he labeled screen time for kids as "digital heroin." Similarly, Jean Twenge has drawn headlines for her criticism of the impact of social media (although, to be fair, her concerns are based on her own fairly solid research).

With every new medium comes concern—and that concern is not necessarily misplaced. Most if not all media have negative aspects as well as positive aspects. The Internet has become like a new Library of Alexandria, with information at people's fingertips: good. But it has also brought with it hate websites, pro-Ana websites, and graphic pornography: not so good. Cell phones have enabled parents to stay in touch with their children and teenagers in unprecedented ways (even through school shootings): good. But cell phones have also resulted in distracted driving, sexting, and cyberbullying: not so good. Sexting and cyberbullying have also represented the worst part of social media, although social networking has also allowed millions of "alternative" or chronically ill youths and adults to find comfort in others.

So worrying about the impact of new media does not represent moral panic as some critics have alleged. Rather it is a legitimate exercise of parental caution and scientific questioning. And yes, there is a world of difference between a dime store novel or a comic book and a first-person shooter video game or graphic online pornography.

For pediatricians, the media represent an important—but not leading—influence on virtually every concern that they, and parents, have about children

growing up: aggressive behavior, violence, sex, drugs, obesity, school performance, sleep, sexting, cyberbullying: the list gets bigger every decade! It may be
reassuring to know that media are not completely responsible for any significant
health problem in children and adolescents. And media can be powerfully useful
and prosocial. On the other hand, it is important for parents, teachers, administrators, and politicians to understand that the media do contribute—sometimes
substantially (e.g., media violence) – to a variety of health issues and concerns.

Let's take a look at a brief summary of the available evidence for media
effects on child and adolescent health. Remember that media research is
extremely difficult to do, is currently under-funded, and far more research is
needed. As a starting point, consider that the last government compendium
on media research was published in 1982 (Pearl et al., 1982), long before the
Internet, cell phones, or social media.

Media violence. Of all the research on media effects, the research on media
violence is both the most voluminous and the most conclusive: children learn
from what they view; and in the case of media violence, they see thousands
of images a year on TV, in movies, and in video games. Once they learn their
attitudes about violence, those attitudes are very difficult to un-learn. The connection between media violence and aggression is actually stronger than the
connections involved in many widely accepted public health risks (figure 1.1):

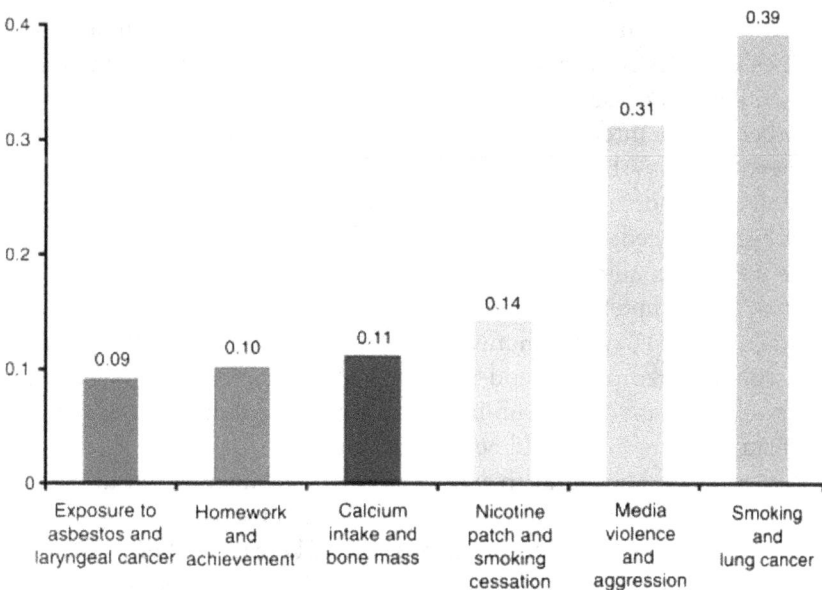

Figure 1.1 Media Violence. Adapted from Bushman and Huesmann (2001). Reprinted
from Strasburger et al. (2014). Copyright ©Sage. Reprinted with permission.

Does that mean that media violence—and first person shooter video games like *Call of Duty* and *Manhunt*—are responsible for school and mass shootings? No. Although increasingly common in the United States, school shootings and mass shootings are still relatively rare; and it would take a population sample of many millions of people to make such a cause-and-effect determination. On the other hand, it is absolutely true that media violence is undoubtedly one contributing factor—one of many, since real-life violence is multifactorial. How big a contribution? Estimates are that media violence contributes 10 percent to real-life violence (Strasburger et al., 2014).

Obesity. As the author of the American Academy of Pediatrics' two-hour rule (children and teens should be limited to no more than two hours/day of entertainment screen time), I can tell you that it was based almost exclusively on the research that links screen time to childhood and adolescent obesity.

Very long-term studies from New Zealand (see chapter 4), Japan, Scotland, and the United States have uniformly found that excessive time spent viewing screens at a young age helps to cause obesity later on (Council on Communications and Media, 2011). Impact varies from study to study, but the risk of obesity is 2–4 times greater with screen time in excess of several hours per day. What is unknown is why: Is it because screen time displaces more active pursuits? The answer is no. Sedentary children tend to remain sedentary, even if you take their screens away.

Sex. Whereas there are hundreds of studies and reports linking media violence to aggressive thoughts and behaviors, there are only 22 longitudinal (i.e., potentially cause-and-effect) studies linking sexual content in media to earlier sexual intercourse; but they almost uniformly find a 2–3 times increased risk (Strasburger, 2020) (figure 1.2).

In addition, there are a hundred studies that document that the media affect kids' knowledge, attitudes, and beliefs about sex and sexuality. Think of the media as a quintessential Sex Educator—especially in the absence of effective and comprehensive sex education in schools.

Drugs. Although a commonly held misperception is that illicit drugs are frequently featured on TV and in movies, it is cigarettes and alcohol (the two most important abused substances for teenagers) that are most common. Marijuana and cocaine would be a distant third.

New research has found that the depiction of smoking and drinking in movies may exceed the influence of parents' use and represent the leading cause of adolescent initiation (Sargent et al., 2012; Stoolmiller et al., 2011). And one study has found that teens who spend a lot of time on social networking sites were five times more likely to use tobacco, three times more

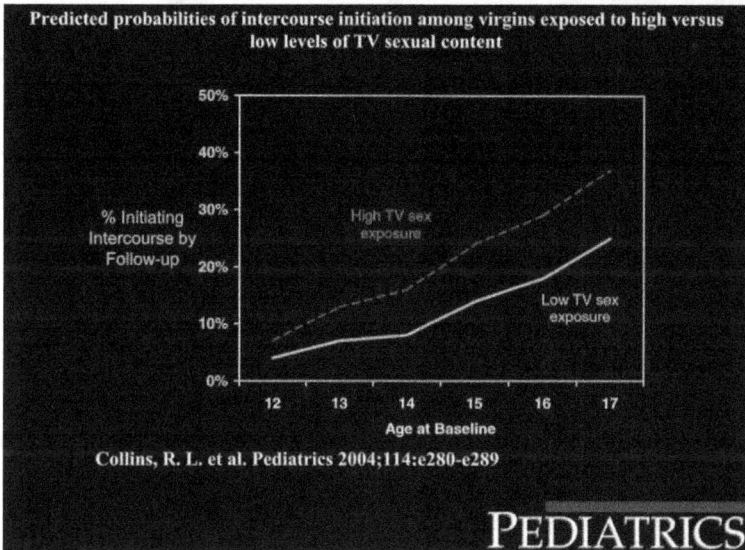

Figure 1.2 TV Sexual Content and Risk of Early Intercourse. Reprinted from https://www.rand.org/pubs/research_briefs/RB9068.html with permission. Copyright © Rand Corporation.

likely to use alcohol, and twice as likely to use marijuana; but it was correlational in design, not longitudinal (National Center on Addiction and Substance Abuse, 2011).

Although tobacco advertising on TV was banned in 1971 by the Public Health Act passed by Congress, more money is currently spent on tobacco marketing and promotion than on alcohol or prescription drugs. To date, the United States and New Zealand are the only countries in the world that allow the advertising of prescription drugs on television.

ADHD and school performance. There are several excellent studies that link media use and ADHD (Christakis et al., 2004; Swing et al., 2010; Zimmerman & Christakis, 2007), but the research literature is still insufficient to draw a firm conclusion. But it was the complaint of teachers in the early years of *Sesame Street* that caused the producers to slow down the pace, and exposing young developing brains to a constant diet of *Spongebob Squarepants* is not likely to be improving their executive function (Lillard & Peterson, 2011).

As far as academic success goes, you would think that it's just common sense that kids who spend a great deal of time with media every day and night might not be succeeding very well in school. The confirmation came with a 2018 study of the parents of 64,464 children ages 6–17 which examined their digital media use and the impact of 5 childhood flourishing factors, primarily academic—completing homework, caring about academics, finishing tasks, staying calm when challenged, and showing interest in learning (Ruest et al., 2018):

- 31% of the kids spent less than 2 hrs/day with media.
- 36% spent 2–4 hrs/day. They were 22% less likely to finish their homework.
- 17% spent 4–6 hrs/day. This group was 46% less likely to finish their homework.
- 16% spent 6 hours or more. This group was 57% less likely to finish their homework.
- The comparative figures held for the other four flourishing factors as well.

Body self-image. If you're the parent or teacher of a pre-teenage or teenage girl, you are probably aware of the fact that the media are not doing you or your child any favors. Several studies have found a possible causal link between exposure to unhealthy body imagery in mainstream media and eating disorders (Becker, 2002; Becker et al., 2011; Hogan & Strasburger, 2008; Martinez-Gonzalez et al., 2003). Pro-Anorexia Nervosa (pro-Ana) websites have proliferated on the Internet—there are now more than 100—and the use of such sites may be predictive of having an eating disorder according to two recent studies (Jett et al., 2010; Peebles et al., 2012).

Depression and suicide (figure 1.3). The number of children and adolescents hospitalized for thoughts of suicide or self-harm has more than doubled in the past 10 years according to data analyzed from 118,363 hospital visits between 2008 and 2015 to 32 children's hospitals. The largest increase was for teenage girls (Morgan et al., 2017). From 2006 to 2016, suicides have increased 70% for white boys ages 10–17 and 77% for black boys according to the CDC (Mercado et al., 2017).

Why this is occurring is an excellent question. Some researchers assert that social media is to blame. What is clear is that portrayals of suicide on TV can sometimes result in a "suicide contagion" that affects teenagers far more than adults.

For decades, researchers have known about the link between media coverage and portrayals of suicide on TV and an increase in actual suicides—a type of "suicide contagion" that affects teens far more than adults (Gould et al., 2003; Romer et al., 2006). So no matter how well intentioned writers

The Teen Suicide Spike
Suicides among 12- to 17-year-olds

Teens are More Depressed
Major Depressive Episodes among
12- to 17-year-olds

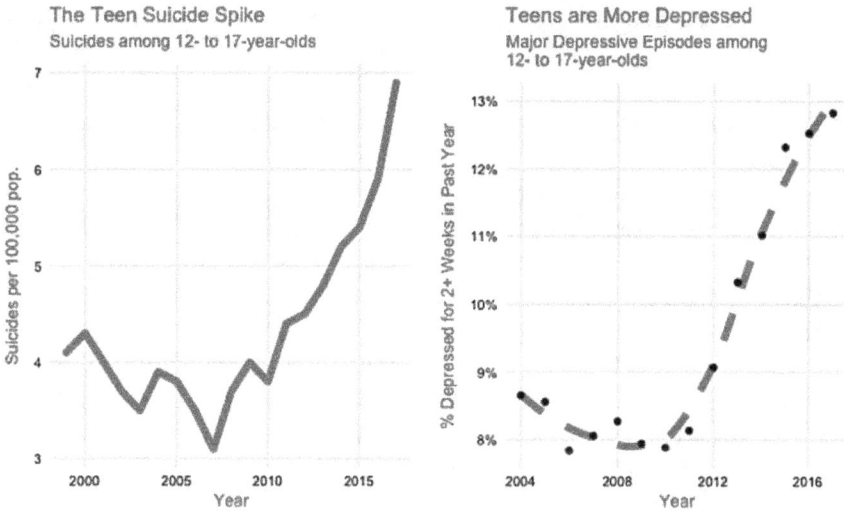

Figure 1.3   Depression and Suicide. CDC Wonder and NSDUH.

and producers are – for example, Netflix's 2017 drama "13 Reasons Why," just aired for a fourth and final season – such programs may have a risk of backfiring unless co-viewed with parents or other adults who actually discuss the content (Brooks, 2017; Zarin-Pass et al., 2018). Excessive media use may also be a marker for depression (Primack et al., 2009b).

Sleep. Teenagers are grumpy enough without being sleep-deprived as well. Schools starting as early as 7:30 a.m. does not help the situation. Mixing a cell phone, a teenager, and a bedroom together is a recipe for disaster. Sleep patterns started getting disrupted with the introduction of smartphones—in 2015, a national survey found that 40% of teens were sleeping less than 7 hours a night, an increase of 58% since 1991 (Twenge et al., 2017).

Very early starting times in high school violate every physiological aspect of adolescent sleep that we know of. Abundant research shows that the average American teenager has difficulty falling asleep before 11 p.m. and ideally wakes up at 8 a.m. or even later (Owens, 2014). School systems like Minneapolis have experimented with later starting times (as late as 9–9:30 a.m.) and found significant improvements in classroom performance and test scores (Wahlstrom et al., 2014).

The American Academy of Pediatrics currently recommends 8–10 hours of sleep for 13–18-year-olds and 9–12 hours for 6–12-year-olds but surveys indicate that most teenagers do not get nearly that amount (Owens, 2014)—less than 10% of students in grades 9–12 in one 2007–2013 study of 12,000—15,000 students (Wheaton et al., 2016). The health consequences can be significant: more risky behaviors and poorer classroom performance and test scores.

Social media. The impact of social networking and social media is a complicated issue (for a full perspective on social media, see volume 2 of this series). The bottom line is the social media are probably like other media in that (a) there are aspects that can be prosocial or negative, (b) there is a dose-response curve to negative media (i.e., more consumption is more problematic), and (c) individual susceptibility to positive or negative effects may vary widely.

There is no question that social networking has allowed certain groups of individuals to find substantial support where they haven't found it previously (e.g., LGBTQ teens, chronically ill teens). But social networking has also brought the twin bugaboos of cyberbullying and sexting to the surface. Studies seem to indicate that teenage anxiety and depression have increased in the past decade: According to researchers examining national rates of self-inflicted injuries (e.g., self-cutting, self-poisoning) between 2001 and 2015, the overall increase was 51%, but for girls ages 10–14, that figure was 166%.

Most of the increase in self-cutting started in 2009, and then continued to increase 18.8% each year (Mercado et al., 2017). This seems to have coincided with the advent of social media according to researchers like Jean Twenge (2017), but whether teen depression and anxiety have increased as a direct result or merely coincidentally is up for debate and further research.

Pro-social effects. Media can be powerfully pro-social. Think *Sesame Street* for young children, *Daniel Tiger's Neighborhood* for toddlers, TV shows like *Glee* and *Cheer* and movies like *Ladybird*, *8th Grade*, *Little Women*, or *Real Women Have Curves* for pre-teens and teenagers. There is not as much research on prosocial effects of media, but they're there (Hogan, 2012). Unfortunately, it sometimes seems like good media are drowned out by potentially harmful media. But important qualities like empathy, tolerance, cooperation, and non-violence can all be increased by pro-social programs (Hogan, 2012).

So is there one medium that predominates? For children (and adults), the answer probably is television (although viewed on many different platforms); for teenagers, social media. But a lot depends on who is using which medium when, for how many hours per day, and how susceptible they may be to media influences.

Conclusion

Are there possible solutions to the negative effects of various media and ways to maximize the prosocial effects of media? Most certainly yes! Below are ten ideas that would both improve media and media's unhealthy impact on children and teenagers.

1. **Minimize guns and interpersonal violence on TV and in movies**. Study after study shows that people like action, but that action doesn't necessarily need to involve gunplay, bones breaking, or heads cracking to be exciting and watchable. Think classic car chase scenes in *Bullit* or *The French Connection*, or the Tyrannosaurus Rex chasing Jeff Goldblum in *Jurassic Park*.

2. **Show healthy sex and sexuality**. Casual sex abounds on primetime TV and in movies with only rare mention of the risks of unprotected sex or the need to use birth control. Arguably, the media deserve a lot of credit for normalizing gay, lesbian, and transgender lifestyles; but they have not done a good job when it comes to public health and sex. Witness the continued lack of birth control (or emergency contraception) advertising on TV.

3. **Stop or decrease the advertising of unhealthy products**. Tobacco product advertising should be banned in all media, and alcohol advertising should be restricted to so-called tombstone advertising, in which the product is shown and discussed in the ad but without the sexy beach babes, talking animals, or humor. Similarly, the advertising of junk food and fast food should be curtailed, particularly when children are targeted. (In 1981, the Federal Trade Commission issued an official government report finding that advertising to children under the age of seven was inherently unfair and deceptive. But it went on to state that since banning such advertising was impractical, never mind.)

4. **Make the funny drunk and the funny "harmless tickle" go away**. More than 80% of movies now contain depictions of alcohol use according to recent research (93% of R-rated films, 72% of PG-13

films, and 46% of G-rated films) (Panko, 2017). Yet there are precious few scenes documenting the harmful effects of alcohol. It's party-time, tipsy people are "drunk as a skunk" but laughing it up, and everyone is drinking and socializing—or alternatively, using a drink to solve their personal problems. Nobody's plowing into a family of five on the highway while they're drunk or even holding their girlfriend's hair while she pukes into the toilet bowl.

Similarly, seemingly everyone is getting baked, toasted, and catching a buzz on TV and in movies (e.g., *Weeds* , *Ted* and *Ted 2*, *High Maintenance*). References to marijuana in popular music are now more common than to alcohol (Hanba & Hanba, 2018). Anytime you make something seem like it's cool and normative behavior, teenagers start to sign on in droves.

5. **Make Media Education mandatory**. It's a shame that Media Education doesn't start with the letter "R," because it belongs right up there with the 3 "R's." Teaching young people how to decipher and use the tsunami of information coming toward them is now just as important as reading, writing, and arithmetic, perhaps even more important. A hundred years ago, to be literate meant that you could read and write. Now it means you can read, write, download, surf, email, text, instant message, and tweet. It also means that you can distinguish between real news and "fake news" (see chapter X).

Several studies have shown that media education can prevent harmful media effects (McCannon, 2014; Moreno et al., 2009; Pinkleton et al., 2008; Primack et al., 2009a). Students can even learn about the dangers of posting sexual references in their social networking profiles and will alter their behavior accordingly (Moreno et al., 2009). They can also be taught that pictures and texts last forever in cyberspace, as ten prospective Harvard students just found out in June, 2017 when Harvard rescinded their admission offers because of offensive images found within a private Facebook group chat. (According to a recent survey of 365 admissions officers around the country, 35% now say that they check applicants' social media profiles (Moody, 2019).

6. **Help schools to learn how to use technology wisely**. While buying iPads instead of textbooks may save thousands of dollars, it may not represent the wisest investment for all students, especially very young students. Many schools now think that simply giving kids access to new

technology is the answer—pass out iPads, open a computer lab, have white-boards in the classroom—all set. But many American schools are 10 years behind when it comes to using media wisely and incorporating new technology into the classroom (Strasburger, 2012).

Yes, times have changed:

The First "Internet Class Goes to College"
How the Class of 2018 Thinks Differently About Things:
1. Amazon has never been just a river in South America.
2. Ferris Bueller and Sloane Peterson could be their parents.
3. They "swipe" cards, not merchandise.
4. "Don't touch that dial!"—what dial?
5. Video games have always had ratings.
6. Music has always been available via free downloads.
7. "PC" means Personal Computer, not Political Correctness.
8. Public schools have always made space available for advertising.

Adapted from http://mindshift/kqed.org/2011/08/the-first-internet-cl ass goes to college/

But new technology isn't always the answer to learning problems. There is far more to LD than ADD or ADHD. Schools need to understand that not only are there alternative learning styles, there are also alternative ways of testing (and understanding) what kids have actually learned.

Unfortunately, Education only seems to have one yardstick with which to measure success—performance on tests, especially standardized tests—thanks to the No Child Left Behind Act. As a result of the 2002 law, new and creative approaches to teaching and learning fall by the wayside unless higher test scores can be documented. This is a prescription for failure and is one of the reasons why American schools are so far behind in teaching students how to adapt to the brave new world of instant technology and connectedness.

7. **End in-person bullying and cyberbullying.** Although in-person bullying remains more common than cyberbullying, the two together add up to an unacceptable number of children and adolescents who are being affected. These days it seems like no child gets out of childhood without either being bullied or bullying someone else. In the 2017 Youth Risk Behavior Survey (YRBS), which involved 14,956 students in grades 9–12 in 144 different schools, 19% reported being bullied at

Sent a Sext
Haven't Sent One

Teens age 12 - 17

Received a Sext
Haven't Received One

Teens age 12 - 17

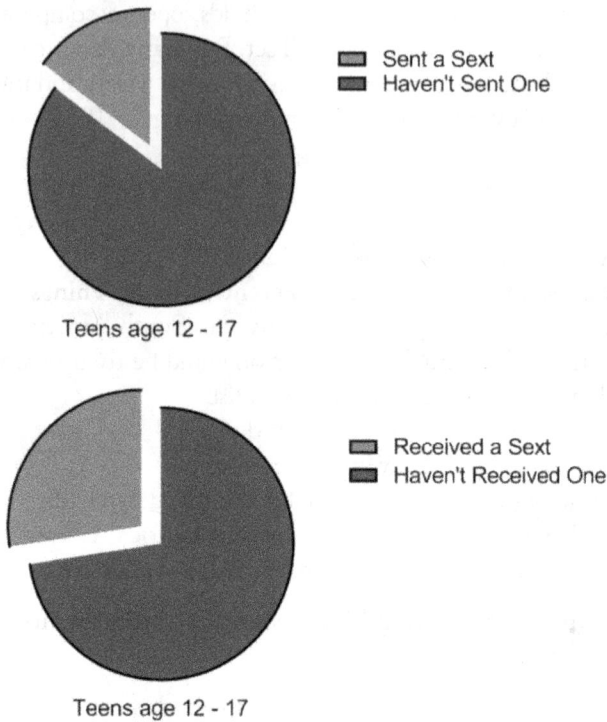

Figure 1.4 Sexting. Data from Madigan et al. (2018). Copyright © F.P. Wilson, M.D. Reprinted with permission. https://www.methodsman.com/blog/teen-sexting.

school and 14.9% reported being bullied electronically (Kann et al., 2018).

A slightly smaller survey but nationally representative survey of 5,600 12–17 year-old students found that 34% had ever been cyberbullied, with 17% saying it had happened within the last 30 days (Florida Atlantic University, 2017).

Not only do schools need to teach "good Internet manners," they now need to monitor or at least screen their students' social media on a regular basis; and there are social media scanning firms which can do exactly that.

8. **Decriminalize sexting**. A recent meta-analysis of 39 different studies found that 1 in 7 teens had sent a sext and 1 in 4 had received one (figure 1.4) (Madigan et al., 2018).

Although obviously unwise and liable to expose teens to charges of child pornography in half of US states, sexting has become a new form of romantic flirting. Teenagers need to be taught that even Snapchat images can be screen-shot and that messages and images last forever in cyberspace. In the absence of media education classes that teach such principles, teenagers should not be held accountable for their dumb behavior (Strasburger et al., 2019).

9. **Help parents to control their children's media use from the get-go.** Many parents are relatively clueless about how media affect their children. On a list of 100 things to argue about with their kids, media use would rank around #136. Of course, the COVID pandemic has made this virtually impossible.

The most common current parenting technique seems to be handing your baby or toddler a cell phone or iPad whenever you want to distract or pacify them. Parents are frequently seen taking their young children to see PG-13 or even R-rated movies. And three-fourths of American children and adolescents report the presence of at least one screen-media device in their bedroom, usually a TV; but half of children had >2 devices in their bedroom at night (Buxton et al., 2015). Approximately 60% reporting regular use of these devices during the hour before bedtime (Hysing et al., 2015). Sometimes overly stressed themselves, parents think that their children are "safe" if they are watching TV or movies in their bedroom.

10. **Increase government investment in media research.**

The last comprehensive government report on media was issued by the National Institute of Mental Health in 1982, long before the Internet, cell phones, or social networking. Virtually no foundations or government agencies currently fund media research, despite the overwhelming importance of media in children's lives and the impact that media have. Congress has occasionally discussed funding more research but never successfully passed legislation that would accomplish that. The only exception is the current ABCD study (Adolescent Brain Cognitive Development), just underway, which has enrolled 10,000 children, ages 9–10 and will follow them for a decade (https://abcdstudy.org/).

Ten relatively simple ideas for the entertainment industry, schools, parents, and the Federal government—but ideas that would make media far healthier for children and teenagers in the coming decades.

References

Anderson, C. A., Gentile, D. A., & Dill, K. E. (2012). Prosocial, antisocial, and other effects of recreational video games. In D. G. Singer & J. L. Singer (Eds.), *Handbook of Children and the Media* (pp. 249–272). Los Angeles, CA: Sage.

Becker, A. E. (2002). Eating behaviours and attitudes following prolonged exposure to television among ethnic Fijian adolescent girls. *British Journal of Psychiatry*, 180, 509–514.

Becker, A. E., Fay, K. E., Agnew-Blais, J., Khan, A. N., Striegel-Moore, R. H., & Gilman, S. E. (2011). Social network media exposure and adolescent eating pathology in Fiji. *British Journal of Psychiatry*, 198, 43–50.

Brooks, M. (2017). Teen suicide experts blast Netflix Series 13 reasons why. *Medscape Pediatrics*, May 5, 2017. Available at: http://www.medscape.com/viewarticle/879606?src=WNL_infoc_170622_MSCPEDIT&uac=5145EZ&impID=1372872&faf=1.

Bushman, B. J., & Huesmann, L. R. (2001). Effects of televised violence on aggression. In D. G. Singer & J. L. Singer (Eds.), *The Handbook of Children and the Media* (pp. 223–254). Thousand Oaks, CA: Sage.

Buxton, OMCA-M., Spilsbury, J. C., Bos, T., Emsellem, H., & Knutson, K. L. (2015). Sleep in the modern family: Protective family routines for child and adolescent sleep. *Sleep Health*, 1, 15–27.

Centers for Disease Control and Prevention. (1994). Guidelines for reporting suicide in the media, 1994. Available at: https://www.cdc.gov/mmwr/preview/mmwrhtml/00031539.htm.

Christakis, D. A., Zimmerman, F. J., DiGiuseppe, D. L., & McCarty, C. A. (2004). Early television exposure and subsequent attentional problems in children. *Pediatrics*, 113(4), 708–713.

Council on Communications and Media, American Academy of Pediatrics. (2011). Children, adolescents, obesity, and the media. *Pediatrics*, 128(1), 201–208.

Florida Atlantic University. (2017). Nationwide teen bullying and cyberbullying study reveals significant issues impacting youth. *ScienceDaily*, February 21, 2017. Available at: https://www.sciencedaily.com/releases/2017/02/170221102036.htm.

Frankel, A. S., Bass, S. B., Patterson, F., Dai, T., & Brown, D. (2018). Sexting, risk behavior, and mental health in adolescents: An examination of 2015 Pennsylvania Youth Risk Behavior Survey data. *Journal of School Health*, 88(3), 190–199.

Gabriel, T., & Richtel, M. (2011). Inflating the software report card. *New York Times*, October 8, 2011. Available at: http://www.nytimes.com/2011/10/09/technology/a-classroom-software-boom-but-mixed-results-despite-the-hype.html?pagewanted=all.

Gould, M., Jamieson, P., & Romer, D. (2003). Media contagion and suicide among the young. *American Behavioral Scientist*, 46, 1269–1284.

Hanba, C., & Hanba, D. (2018). Opioid and drug prevalence in Top 40's music: A 30 year review. *The Journal of the American Board of Family Medicine*, 31(5), 761–767.

Hogan, M. (2012). Prosocial effects of media. *Pediatric Clinics*, 59(3), 635–645.

Hogan, M. J., & Strasburger, V. C. (2008). Body image, eating disorders, and the media. *Adolescent Medicine: State of the Art Reviews*, 19, 521–546.

Hysing, M., Pallesen, S., Stormark, K. M., Jakobsen, R., Lundervold, A. J., & Sivertsen, B. (2015). Sleep and use of electronic devices in adolescence: Results from a large population-based study. *BMJ Open*, 5, e006748. DOI: 10.1136/bmjopen-2014-006748.

Jett, S., LaPorte, D. J., & Wanchisn, J. (2010). Impact of exposure to pro-eating disorder websites on eating behavior in college women. *European Eating Disorder Reviews*, 18, 410–416.

Kann, L., McManus, T., & Harris, W. A. (2018). Youth risk behavior surveillance—United States, 2017. *MMWR Surveillance Summary*, 67(No. SS-#8), 1–479.

Lillard, A. S., & Peterson, J. (2011). The immediate impact of different types of television on young children's executive function. *Pediatrics*, 128(4), 644–649.

Madigan, S., Ly, A., Rash, C. L., Van Ouytsel, J., & Temple, J. R. (2018). Prevalence of multiple forms of sexting behavior among youth. *JAMA Pediatrics*, 172(4), 327–335.

Martinez-Gonzalez, M. A., Gual, P., Lahortiga, F., Alonso, Y., de Irala-Estévez, J., & Cervera, S. (2003). Parental factors, mass media influences, and the onset of eating disorders in a prospective population-based cohort. *Pediatrics*, 111, 315–320.

Marynak, K., Gentzke, A., Wang, T. W., Neff, L., & King, B. A. (2018). Exposure to electronic cigarette advertising among middle and high school students—United States, 2014–2016. *MMWR Morbidity and Mortality Weekly Report*, 67, 294–299. DOI: 10.15585/mmwr.mm6710a3.

McCannon, B. (2014). Media literacy/media education. In V. C. Strasburger, B. J. Wilson, & A. Jordan (Eds.), *Children, Adolescents, the Media* (3rd ed., pp. 507–558). Thousand Oaks, CA: Sage.

McKnight-Eily, L. R., Eaton, D. K., Lowry, R., Croft, J. B., Presley-Cantrell, L., & Perry, G. S. (2011). Relationships between hours of sleep and health-risk behaviors in US adolescent students. *Preventive Medicine*, 53(4–5), 271–273.

Mercado, M., Holland, K., & Leemis, R. W. (2017). Trends in emergency department visits for nonfatal self-inflicted injuries among youth aged 10 to 24 years in the United States, 2001–2015. *JAMA*, 318, 1931–1933.

Moody, J. (2019). Why colleges look at students' social media. *U.S. News & World Report*. Available at: https://www.usnews.com/education/best-colleges/articles /2017-02-10/colleges-really-are-looking-at-your-social-media-accounts.

Moreno, M. A., VanderStoep, A., Parks, M. R., Zimmerman, F. J., Kurth, A., & Christakis, D. A. (2009). Reducing at-risk adolescents' display of risk behavior on a social networking web site. *Archives of Pediatrics and Adolescent Medicine*, 163, 35–41.

Morgan, C., Webb, R. T., Carr, M. J., Kontopantelis, E., Green, J., Chew-Graham, C. A., ... & Ashcroft, D. M. (2017). Incidence, clinical management, and mortality risk following self harm among children and adolescents: Cohort study in primary care. *British Medical Journal*, 359, j4351.

National Center on Addiction and Substance Abuse. (2011). *National Survey of American Attitudes on Substance Abuse XVI: Teens and Parents*. New York, NY: Columbia University. Available at: http://www.casacolumbia.org/upload/2011/20110824teensurveyreport.pdf.

Owens, J., & Adolescent Sleep Working Group, & Committee on Adolescence. (2014). Insufficient sleep in adolescents and young adults: An update on causes and consequences. *Pediatrics*, 134(3), e921–e932.

Panko, B. (2017). From Budweiser to Heineken, alcohol brands are rampant in Hollywood films. *Smithsonian Magazine*. Available at: http://www.smithsonianmag.com/science-nature/budweiser-heineken-alcohol-brands-are-now-rampant-hollywood-films-180963207/.

Pearl, D., Bouthilet, L., & Lazar, J. (1982). *Television and Behavior: Ten Years of Scientific Progress and Implications for the Eighties*. Rockville, MD: National Institute of Mental Health.

Peebles, R., Wilson, J. L., Litt, I. F., Hardy, K. K., Lock, J. D., Mann, J. R., & Borzekowski, D. L. (2012). Disordered eating in a digital age: Eating behaviors, health, and quality of life in users of websites with pro-eating disorder content. *Journal of Medical Internet Research*, 14, e148.

Pinkleton, B. E., Austin, E. W., Cohen, M., Chen, Y. C. Y., & Fitzgerald, E. (2008). Effects of a peer-led media literacy curriculum on adolescents' knowledge and attitudes toward sexual behavior and media portrayals of sex. *Health Communication*, 23(5), 462–472.

Primack, B. A., Sidani, J., Carroll, M. V., & Fine, M. J. (2009a). Associations between smoking and media literacy in college students. *Journal of Health Communication*, 14(6), 541–555.

Primack, B. A., Swanier, B., Georgiopoulos, A. M., Land, S. R., & Fine, M. J. (2009b). Association between media use in adolescence and depression in young adulthood: A longitudinal study. *Archives of General Psychiatry*, 66, 181–188.

Romer, D., Jamieson, P. E., & Jamieson, K. H. (2006). Are news reports of suicide contagious? A stringent test in six US cities. *Journal of Communication*, 56(2), 253–270.

Ruest, S., Gjelsvik, A., Rubinstein, M., & Amanullah, S. (2018). The inverse relationship between digital media exposure and childhood flourishing. *Journal of Pediatrics*, 197, 268–274.

Sargent, J. D., Tanski, S., & Stoolmiller, M. (2012). Influence of motion picture rating on adolescent response to movie smoking. *Pediatrics*, 130(2), 228–236.

Stoolmiller, M., Wills, T. A., McClure, A. C., Tanski, S. E., Worth, K. A., Gerrard, M., & Sargent, J. D. (2011). Comparing media and family predictors of alcohol use: A cohort study of US adolescents. *BMJ Open*, 2(1). DOI: 10.1136/bmjopen-2011-000543.

Strasburger, V. C. (2012). School daze: Why are schools so clueless about the media? *Pediatric Clinics of North America*, 59(3), 705–715.

Strasburger, V. C. (2020). *The Death of Childhood: Reinventing the Joy of Growing Up.* Cambridge, MA: Cambridge Scholars Press.

Strasburger, V. C., Wilson, B. J., & Jordan, A. (2014). *Children, Adolescents, and the Media* (3rd ed.). Thousand Oaks, CA: Sage.

Strasburger, V. C., Zimmerman, H., Temple, J. E., & Madigan, S. (2019). Teenagers, sexting, & the law. *Pediatrics*, 143(5), e20183183. DOI: 10.1542/peds.2018-3183.

Swing, E. L., Gentile, D. A., Anderson, C. A., & Walsh, D. A. (2010). Television and video game exposure and the development of attention problems. *Pediatrics*, 126, 214–221.

Twenge, J. (2017). *iGen: Why Today's Super-Connected Kids Are Growing Up Less Rebellious, More Tolerant, Less Happy—and Completely Unprepared for Adulthood—and What That Means for the Rest of Us.* New York: Atria Books.

Twenge, J. M., Krizan, Z., & Hisler, G. (2017). Decreases in self-reported sleep duration among U.S. adolescents 2009–2015 and association with new media screen time. *Sleep Medicine*, 39, 47–53.

Van Geel, M., Vedder, P., & Tanilon, J. (2014). Relationship between peer victimization, cyberbullying, and suicide in children and adolescents: A meta-analysis. *JAMA Pediatrics*, 168, 435–442.

Wahlstrom, K. (2010). School start time and sleepy teens. *Archives of Pediatric and Adolescent Medicine*, 164, 676–677.

Wahlstrom, K., Dretzke, B., Gordon, M., Peterson, K., Edwards, K., & Gdula, J. (2014). Examining the impact of later high school start times on the health and academic performance of high school students: A multi-site study. Available at: https://conservancy.umn.edu/handle/11299/162769.

Wheaton, A. G., Olsen, E. O. M., Miller, G. F., & Croft, J. B. (2016). Sleep duration and injury-related risk behaviors among high school students—United States, 2007–2013. *Morbidity and Mortality Weekly Report*, 65(13), 337–341.

Zarin-Pass, M., Plager, P., & Pitt, M. B. (2018). 13 Things pediatricians should know (and do) about *13 Reasons Why. Pediatrics*, 141(6), e20180575. DOI: 10.1542/peds.2018-0575.

Zimmerman, F. J., & Christakis, D. A. (2007). Associations between content types of early media exposure and attentional problems. *Pediatrics*, 120, 986–992.

CHAPTER 2

~

The 7 +/- 2 Deadly Sins of Video Game Violence Research

El-Lim Kim, Craig A. Anderson, Douglas A. Gentile

Introduction

After taking into consideration numerous characteristics of the child and the environment, including risk and protective factors, research clearly shows that media violence consumption increases the relative risk of aggression. (Media Violence Commission, International Society for Research on Aggression, 2012)

Many factors are known to be risk factors for increased aggressive behavior, aggressive cognition and aggressive affect, and reduced prosocial behavior, empathy and moral engagement, and violent video game use is one such risk factor. (American Psychological Association, 2015)

Researchers found there was a significant association between exposure to media violence and aggressive behavior, aggressive thoughts, angry feelings, and physiological arousal. (American Academy of Pediatrics, Committee on Communication and Media, 2016)

Does playing violent video games lead to aggression and violence? The controversy on the harmful effects of violent video games still persists. Game industries claim that it is a both a fact and a common sense that video games are not related to violence (Entertainment Software Association, 2019). Some critics of video game violence research also argue that video games have been wrongly scapegoated for violent real-life incidents such as mass shootings, and that video games should not be blamed for real-life violence (Ferguson, 2019).

Nonetheless, studies from the behavioral sciences consistently reveal that violent video games significantly increase the risk of aggressive behavior, aggressive thinking, and aggressive feelings, and that media violence in general has similar effects (Anderson et al., 2003, 2010; Mathur & Vander-Weele, 2019; Prescott et al., 2018). Indeed, every major comprehensive review by scientific societies yields the same conclusion as that offered in the opening epigraphs. For a list of such reports, see http://www.craiganderson. org/wp-content/uploads/caa/StatementsonMediaViolence.html).

Amid such mixed opinions, one may wonder: Why do these controversies exist? This chapter focuses on why (and how) some research studies fail to find significant violent video game effects on aggression. By examining key reasons behind a "no effect" conclusion, this chapter also provides guidelines for how such controversies in many scientific domains could be resolved.

Why Such Controversies Exist

Evidence Based on the Three Main Types of Scientific Studies

Many arguments about violent video games and aggression center on scientific studies, mainly from the disciplines of social sciences. There are different ways to study the effects of video game violence. In most cases, researchers conduct one of three types of studies: in-lab experimental studies, questionnaire-based cross-sectional studies, or long-term studies that look into changes in video game effects over time.

Experiments. Experimental studies usually are conducted in controlled laboratory settings. In a typical violent video game experiment, participants are randomly assigned to play a violent (e.g., *Grand Theft Auto*) or a nonviolent video game (e.g., *Pinball 3D*).[1] After the participants finish playing the assigned video game(s), participants are mildly provoked and then given an opportunity to behave aggressively. If the group that played the violent video game behaves more aggressively than the group that played a nonviolent video game, researchers can infer that the violent video game has *caused* an increase in aggression because the game is the only factor that was different between the groups.

A team of researchers led by Gabbiadini (2014) conducted an experimental study that looked into the causal relationship between violent video game play and aggression. The researchers randomly assigned high school students into two different groups: (1) violent video game group (*GTA San Andreas* or *GTA III*), or: (2) nonviolent video game group (*Pinball 3D* or *Mini golf 3D*). The participants were told that the objective of the research was to investigate whether playing video games could influence their cognitive abilities.

A cover story like this is often used to reduce suspicion and bias in responding. In fact, the "cognitive abilities" task measured aggressive behavior.

Participants practiced and then played their assigned game for 45 minutes. Afterwards, the participants' aggression level was measured using the competitive reaction time task (CRTT), which is a commonly used, well-validated measure of aggression (e.g., Bartholow & Anderson, 2002; Giancola & Parrott, 2008; Hyatt et al., 2019; Konijn et al., 2007; Taylor, 1967). When used correctly, participants in CRTT studies are told that they will play a game against another person. The game consists of several reaction time contests, in which the winner can deliver an obnoxious noise blast to the loser. The winner chooses how loud the noise blast is, ranging from no noise at all to painfully loud.

In actuality, there is no real opponent; the computer determines which "contests" the participant loses (and thereby is blasted by the fake opponent) and wins (and thereby can blast the fake opponent). Giving loud noise blasts to the opponent is a safe form of aggressive behavior. In this study, the researchers found that those who played violent video games delivered significantly louder noise blasts than those who played nonviolent video games. Thus, it could be concluded that violent video games increased aggressive behavior in this short-term setting.

Cross-sectional correlational studies. Another common method is questionnaire-based cross-sectional studies. Participants (and sometimes parents, peers, or teachers) complete a set of questionnaires that include at least one measure of violent video game exposure and one measure of the participants' tendency to behave aggressively. The questionnaires usually gather additional information about the participants, such as gender, socioeconomic status (SES), and parental relationship to see whether theoretically relevant variables are also related to violent game playing.

Siyez and Baran (2017) surveyed 318 middle school students to determine whether frequency of playing violent video games was associated with aggressive behaviors. Students reported their three favorite games and completed an aggression questionnaire that asked whether they have previously engaged in a list of aggressive behaviors, such as having a gang fight. The researchers categorized the games reported by the students as "prosocial," "neutral," or "aggressive." The results showed that students who frequently played at least one violent game were more likely to engage in aggressive behaviors than those who did not play such games.

Cross-sectional studies allow researchers to understand associations between violent video games, aggression, and other measured variables. By themselves, such studies do not prove that violent game play *causes* increased aggression. In any specific study of this type, it is entirely possible that factors such as growing up in a poor family might cause a person to become both highly aggressive and to prefer violent video games over others.

Nonetheless, sets of cross-sectional studies that test theoretically-based alternative explanations (such as low SES) can lend strength to the violent-games-increase-aggression hypothesis, but more importantly, they also can contradict a causal hypothesis if no theoretically-predicted relation is found.

Longitudinal. Longitudinal studies often are similar to cross-sectional ones, in that various measures of video game habits, aggressive behaviors, and other theoretically relevant characteristics are assessed about the participants. They are often by self-reports, but also by parents, teachers, police records and so on, in the same way as cross-sectional studies. However, in longitudinal studies the key measures (such as aggressive behaviors in the past six months) are measured repeatedly over time (from several months to years).

The main goal of longitudinal studies is to see how people change, to help address which changes in variables come before others (and therefore remain plausible causes). Longitudinal studies, therefore, can help to answer the "chicken-and-egg" question. Specifically, such a study might see whether people who play violent video games become more aggressive as time passes, even after statistically controlling for how aggressive they were earlier in their lives. In this way, longitudinal studies can do a better job at testing whether or not habitual violent game play causes later aggressive behavior tendencies.

Gentile et al. (2014) assessed 3,034 children and adolescents from Singapore over three years. Among other measures, participants reported gaming habits, aggressive behaviors, and aggressive cognitions three times. High amounts of violent game play in year 1 predicted increased aggressive thoughts, which in turn predicted increased aggressive behaviors at year three, supporting the hypothesized causal long-term effect of violent video games on aggression. Obviously, we know that aggressive behavior at year three could not cause amount of violent gaming at year one, which eliminates the ambiguity about causal direction inherent in most cross-sectional studies.

Summary of evidence. This section has briefly described and given examples of the three main types of research used by scientists to study how violent video play may be related to aggressive behavior. Keep in mind that no single study (in psychology or any other science) can definitively answer all key causal questions. The strongest evidence that some environmental feature causes a specific outcome—such as smoking causing lung cancer—requires multiple studies using different methods that, despite their differences, still converge on the same finding.

Substantial numbers of research studies of different types have converged on the finding that there is a causal effect of violent game play on aggression for children and adolescents (AAP Committee on Communications and Media, 2016; APA Task Force on Violent Media, 2015; Calvert et al., 2017; Media Violence Commission, International Society for Research on Aggression, 2012). A much smaller research literature shows similar convergence on the link between media violence and violent behavior (e.g., Anderson et al., 2010).

However, as noted at the beginning of this chapter, some scholars (and companies that sell violent media) assert that there is no causal relationship between violent video games and aggression or violence. They often back this assertion by citing a few research studies that have found no effect. If playing violent video games in general leads to an increase in aggression, how can there be studies that do not show such an effect? The next section presents seven possible "sins" committed by researchers that could lead to a "no effect" finding.

How to Be Critical of the Critical Position Science grows through critical examination. "Critical" means thoughtful assessments of the strengths and weaknesses of the research literature, not nasty comments about studies or researchers. Critical assessments of existing media violence research have helped make the research base stronger.

Nonetheless, there is a need to be critical of the critics, and not assume that all criticisms are equally valid. There are numerous flaws with some of the arguments used to deny that violent screen media (including video games) can increase the likelihood of aggressive behavior. What follows is not an exhaustive list, but this list can help to make examination of the science more accurate.

Several introductory points must be kept in mind. First, in any field of science, not all studies will produce the same results. Even the most well-established causal relations (e.g., smoking and lung cancer) do not appear in all studies. A study that fails to find the same effect that most studies find does not disprove that effect. It does invite close examination of both that study and of the larger research literature, but it cannot be seen as conclusive.

Second, one of the reasons for variability in results is that in every study there is a degree of randomness (or error) in the measurement of key variables, in the selection of research participants, even sometimes in the assignment of participants to experimental conditions.

Third, some studies are poorly designed, poorly executed, poorly ana-lyzed, and/or poorly interpreted. This third reason characterizes many of the studies that those who most vociferously deny the effects use as support for their position. This chapter summarizes a number of these commonalities as "Seven Deadly Sins" in media violence research.[2]

Sin 1: Small Sample Size

One common reason for failure to find a statistically significant effect of video game violence is use of a too-small sample size. A study of three smok-ers and three nonsmokers cannot conclusively prove or disprove whether or not smoking causes cancer. A study with a small sample size is considered *underpowered*; it lacks the ability to accurately assess whether there is truly an effect.

In a sense, a small sample size is like using just your eyes or a hand-held magnifying glass to look for micro-organisms in a drop of pond water. Just because you cannot see them does not mean that they are not there. Alterna-tively, a large sample size is like using a microscope to look for small objects.

Given the likely size of the media violence effect that has been docu-mented across several meta-analyses (e.g., Anderson et al., 2010; Ferguson, 2007), the minimum sample size needed for an experiment is 100 people per condition—that is, if you are testing a violent game compared to a nonviolent game, the *minimum* needed is 200. If you are further interested in whether boys are more affected by violent games than girls (or if younger children are more affected than older children), the number of participants needs to be more than doubled for each of these additional considerations in order to have high confidence in the study results (e.g., sufficient statistical power).

The same sample size deadly sin applies to cross-sectional and longitudi-nal studies as well. Generally speaking, cross-sectional studies of video game effects should include at least 200 participants, and longitudinal studies should have even more.

Many studies that fail to find significant results have samples that are much too small, which is surprising because the strength of the media vio-lence effect (i.e., the effect size) is widely known, so that the researchers could have considered having a larger sample size for a more accurate assess-ment. It could be difficult in a practical world to have studies of 200–1000 participants. Yet the odds of a null result skyrocket without a sufficient sample size, not because there is no effect, but just because there is not suf-ficient statistical power to find it. This is not, however, the only problem with small sample sizes.

Consider a hypothetical example: suppose a researcher recruited 10 participants and randomly assigned them (with a coin toss) to play either a violent or a nonviolent game for a few minutes, after which they complete a CRTT aggression measure. Suppose the results show that the violent game condition participants behaved slightly less aggressively than those in the nonviolent game condition, but not significantly so.

Does this study result demonstrate that violent game play does not affect aggression? Is it not possible that just by chance, four of the five participants in the nonviolent game condition were people who typically aggress against others whenever possible, and that only two of the five in the nonviolent game condition were high aggressive individuals? Is it likely that the coin toss did not "equalize" the two groups prior to the experimental manipulation of which game they played?

The answer is yes; it is quite possible for this to happen, just as it is quite possible to get four heads out of five tosses of a coin. Thus, even if the truth is that playing a violent video game increases aggression for a brief period of time, a small-sample study may fail to find such an effect because of the randomization failure combined with the fact that trait aggressiveness (e.g., average everyday level of aggression) leads to relatively more aggression in most situations.[3]

In contrast, large sample sizes reduce the likelihood of such randomization failures. For example, you are much less likely to get 80% heads when you toss a fair coin 200 times than when you toss it only 10 times. Similar sample size problems exist with cross-sectional and longitudinal research as well, problems involving sampling bias, measurement error, and other issues too boring and technical for this short chapter.

In sum, researchers and consumers of research must be careful when interpreting results from studies that employ small sample sizes. Small-sample studies should not be totally ignored either, because their results can be combined with the findings of other similar studies using *meta-analysis* techniques; the resulting larger *combined* samples can be informative. Over-interpreting single studies with small samples, however, is a common deadly scientific sin.

Sin 2. Inappropriate Experimental Stimuli
A second common reason for null effects results from poor selection of games to compare in experiments. As discussed previously, researchers conducting an experimental study randomly assign participants into at least two conditions: a violent game or a nonviolent game condition. In some studies, violent and nonviolent games conditions have been mismatched, such that the

so-called nonviolent games did in fact contain considerable violent content (e.g., Brady & Mathews, 2006; Elson et al., 2015; Tear & Nielsen, 2014).

For example, some researchers might choose a nonviolent game based on the game's industry-based rating as being appropriate for children, rather than on actual content in the game. In reality, the majority of popular "children's" and "teen" games have a lot of violent content (defined as characters trying to harm other characters; Gentile, 2008). In studies that use industry ratings instead of actual violent content, it is not surprising that the two experimental conditions do not yield different levels of aggression, because in both conditions the participants played games with violent content. In other words, there was no real nonviolent game control group.

Sin 3. A Poor Cover Story/No Suspicion Check

Ensuring that research participants remain ignorant of the true research purpose (i.e., violent video game effect on aggression) is crucial in obtaining valid results. One study found that participants who play a lot of violent video games, and therefore want to believe that there are no harmful effects, behaved less aggressively in the study when it was obvious that the study was about gaming and aggression than when they didn't know that (Bender et al., 2013).

In other words, gamers who would feel uncomfortable believing in a harmful effect of violent video games may purposely distort their behavior (including rating scales) in such a way to minimize the effect, if they know or guess the true purpose of the study. To prevent such response bias, researchers must use an adequate cover story to make sure that participants are not aware of the true research hypothesis.

Recall that in the study by Gabbiadini et al. (2014) the participants were told that the purpose of the study was to examine the relationship between video games and cognitive abilities (whereas, in fact, it was to see whether violent video games increase to aggression), and that they would play a competitive reaction time game afterwards (which is actually used to measure aggression); these are examples of a cover story.

Unfortunately, sometimes researchers are not very clever in concealing the true research purpose, by use of a poor cover story, or even worse, by revealing the true purpose in the study title ("Violent video game effects on aggression") or in the consent form. Some of the most-cited null-results studies don't even report whether a cover story was used, let alone participant suspicion about the purpose of the study.

A study could be poorly executed even if there is a cover story. Having a cover story is not sufficient, because there often will be participants who are suspicious, especially since game research has often been the subject of popular discussion and debate.

For this reason, researchers need to assess suspicion, perhaps by questioning participants after they complete the study. If it turns out that a substantial portion knew or guessed the real purpose, the whole study becomes uninterpretable. If it is an only a small subset who guessed the purpose of the study, tests can be performed to see whether suspicion invalidates the results.

Sin 4. (Wrong) Variables Are Measured (Wrongly)

Another way to "ruin" a research study is to use poor measures. There are several versions of this problem. Many studies rely heavily on questionnaires, and many must be administered within a tight time schedule. Therefore, researchers like to keep questionnaires brief. This becomes a problem when too few questionnaire items are used to measure key variables.

For example, using one, two, or even five-question measures of violent game experience (e.g., "How violent is your favorite game?) tend to yield weak measures of the complex concept "violent video game exposure." Several standard and well-validated measures exist, each of which includes sets of specific questions that adequately assess violent video game exposure (see Busching et al., 2015). The same "too few items" problem applies to all concepts one wishes to measure, including aggression.

Similarly, researchers sometimes fail to measure the most appropriate variable. For example, some failed studies did not measure violent game exposure at all, but instead only assessed total time spent playing any type (violent or nonviolent) of game. It doesn't matter how many items are used in this case; if the items don't measure the correct variable, the measure is invalid for the intended purpose.

A more subtle version of failing to measure the most appropriate variable often appears in measures of aggression. Theoretically, violent video games should have a larger impact on physical aggression (e.g., hitting other people) than on relational aggression (e.g., spreading rumors). The type of aggression most commonly modeled in violent games is physical, not relational. Therefore, studies that measure the wrong type of aggression or that muddle the measure by averaging a few physical aggression items with other types of items are likely to underestimate the true violent game effects.

One article frequently cited by video game effects deniers used one item, "arguing with friends" to measure aggression (Williams & Skoric, 2005). Such a measure fails to meet minimum standards for several reasons, including: (1) theoretically, aggression is defined as behavior *intended* to hurt the other person, and friends usually argue without intent to actually harm their friend; (2) violent games most often model physical, not verbal aggression; and (3) it has too few items to yield a reliable measure.

A more recent null-effect article used as an aggression measure a scale that had been developed by other scholars to measure "strengths and difficulties," but not aggression (Przybylski & Weinstein, 2019). Most of the items on this measure clearly were not measures of aggression. A recent reanalysis of that data set using more appropriate measures and analyses found the opposite effect, that violent video game exposure was positively associated with aggressive behavior (Miles-Novelo & Anderson, in preparation).

Yet another common mistake is the use of a generally accepted measure of aggression but in the wrong context (e.g., Teng et al., 2011). Trait measures are designed to assess stable general personality tendencies, not moment-to-moment states and behaviors. Playing a violent video game for 20 minutes should not increase how many physical fights the participant had been in during the past 6 months, but this error in using trait-like measures of aggression in a short-term context has happened frequently in null effect studies.

A final example concerns inappropriate use of extremely rare acts of aggression. Being convicted of violent crimes, as shown in police records, is quite rare for most of the populations that have been studied (e.g., children, college students). Thus, detecting a "significant" effect of violent game exposure on violent crime would require huge sample sizes, maybe 100,000, even if there is a true effect.

Of course, one can't actually conduct experimental studies of violent games on truly violent behavior, because one cannot ethically conduct such studies. Imagine trying to do a study in which 3rd graders are randomly assigned to play a violent or nonviolent video game for 30 minutes, and then are given handguns and an hour of recess time so that the researcher can see which group shoots the most classmates.[4]

Interestingly, large sample cross-sectional and longitudinal studies of media violence and violent behavior have found significant effects on actual violent behavior (e.g., DeLisi et al., 2012; Exelmans et al., 2015; Hull et al., 2014). These studies tend to have very large samples and to use populations at risk for violent behavior.

Sin 5. Statistical Errors

There are hundreds of different ways to conduct a statistical analysis. This is because there are also hundreds of different types of data. Characteristics of the data could differ based on how the scores are dispersed and whether the scoring range is restricted, etc.

Suppose a group of researchers asked 150 people to indicate how often they showed their anger when they are frustrated, with possible answers ranging from "never" to "always." Most of the respondents will report that they show their anger *some* of the times, with only a few reporting *never* or *always*, resulting in a score distribution that looks like the first graph (see figure 2.1).

On the other hand, if the researchers ask 150 people to report how many times they have been arrested for criminal assaults, a vast majority of them will report that they have *never* been arrested, creating a score distribution like the second graph (see figure 2.2).

As shown, the spread of the scores can differ drastically depending on the variable being measured. Different statistical analyses should be used to address such differences in data characteristics. However, sometimes researchers fail to acknowledge different data characteristics and use a statistical analysis that does not best fit the data, which may contribute to distorted research findings.

Furthermore, researchers who conduct questionnaire-based cross-sectional studies often collect additional information from the respondents, such as gender and parental relationship. This is because researchers want to statistically test whether violent video game play would still be associated with aggression when these other variables are taken into consideration (that is, have been statistically "controlled"). However, researchers often make mistakes by choosing the wrong variables to control.

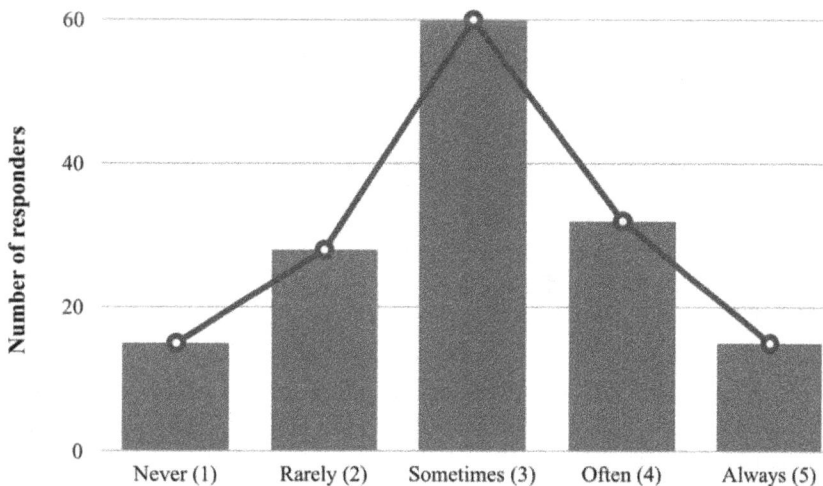

Figure 2.1   Score Distribution for Anger.

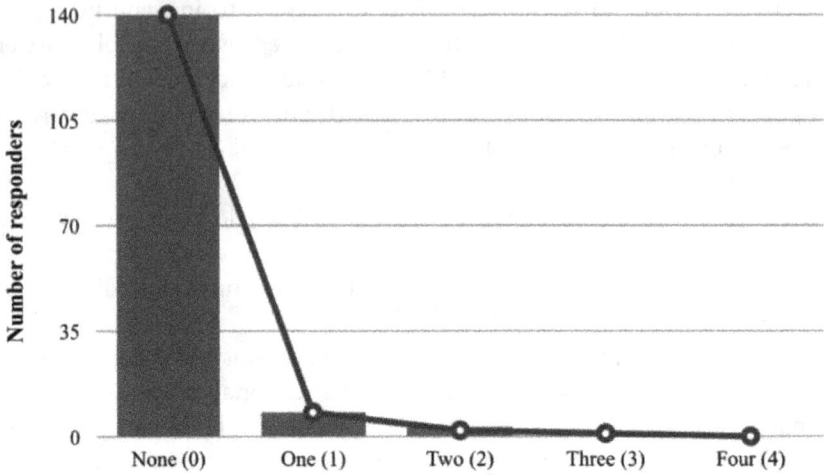

Figure 2.2   Score Distribution for Criminal Assaults.

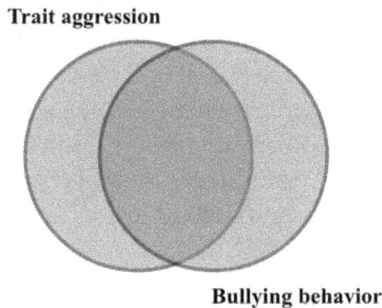

Figure 2.3a   Relationship between Trait Aggression and Bullying Behavior.

One such mistake can be made when the researchers choose a variable that is closely related to aggression. Consider the Venn diagram representing the relations between violent game play, trait aggression (general aggressive tendencies) and bullying behaviors in figure 2.3. Areas of overlap within the circles represent the size of association (or correlation) of the variables.

Bullies are usually aggressive, because bullying behaviors include different kinds of aggressive behaviors such as hitting, pushing, taunting, threatening, and spreading hurtful rumors (Salmivalli, 2010). Therefore, one should expect there to be a close relationship between trait aggression and bullying behaviors, as illustrated by the large overlapping area in figure 2.3a.

What about the relation between video game violence and bullying behaviors while taking trait aggression into consideration (i.e., statistically controlling for it)? Because trait aggression and bullying behaviors are very closely related (remember, they both include the same kinds of aggressive behaviors), their association with video game violence will also be similar.

Hence, if researchers "control" for trait aggression when examining the relationship between video game violence and bullying, the observed relationship between the two would be artificially smaller than what it should be (marked by area labeled α_3 in figure 2.3b), because the researchers are now excluding the association shared by trait aggression and bullying behaviors with video game violence (see area labeled α_2 in figure 2.3b).

This does not yield an accurate depiction of the relationship, because the true relationship should be larger (the sum of both area α_3 and α_2 in figure 2.3b). In other words, by controlling for one measure of aggression, the researcher essentially has tested whether the effect of violent games on aggression measure 1 is significant after controlling for aggression measure 2.

As shown, choosing the wrong variable as a "control" can greatly change the outcome of a study. Indeed, the most appropriate test of whether video game violence is related to aggression in this particular cross-sectional study is the sum of α_1, α_2 and α_3 in figure 2.3b. By considering only α_3, the researcher has thrown out the baby with the bath water. Most researchers know this, but this statistical technique can be used to incorrectly make it appear that there is no relation when in fact there is.

Another way researchers can make a mistake when selecting the variables to control is to choose a variable that theoretically explains the link between video game violence and aggression (called a *mediating variable*).

For example, research and theory shows that habitually playing violent video games can increase physical aggression *because* repeated violent game

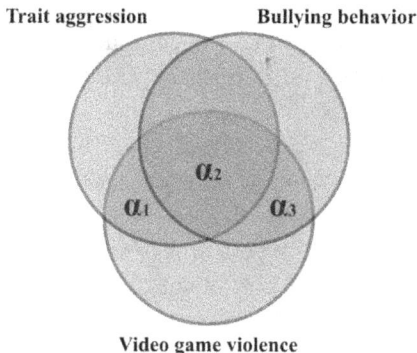

Figure 2.3b   Relationship between Video Game Violence and Trait Aggression, When Bullying Behavior Is Put Into Consideration.

play influences internal psychological factors that are themselves directly linked to the risk of aggression, such as the belief that it is acceptable to use aggression, or the tendency to think that other people are out to get them (i.e., video game violence → aggressive thoughts → aggressive behaviors).

Therefore, researchers should not control the mediating variable (aggressive thoughts) when analyzing the relationship between video game violence and aggressive behaviors, because the aggressive thoughts variable is a causal link between video game violence exposure and aggressive behaviors (Anderson et al., 2007; Möller & Krahé, 2009).

Researchers can also make a statistical mistake by controlling a variable that is closely related to the main predictor variable of interest. Research shows that children who are exposed to a lot of video game violence also tend to be exposed to a lot of television violence. Because of this overlap, "controlling" for television violence in statistical analyses is not optimal, because this process inappropriately minimizes the observed effect of video game violence on aggression.

These are not the only statistical errors that can be made, but they are the most typical in this area.[5]

Sin 6. Conceptual Errors

A commonly heard argument against violent game research goes as follows: "My friends and I have been playing violent video games for years and we haven't shot anyone!" This is likely a true statement; media violence by itself does not turn normal, well-adjusted children into blood-thirsty murderers.

One common public misconception is that mainstream media violence researchers claim that children will become school shooters or mass murderers from playing violent video games. This is the result of false dramatization by the popular media, which often quote politicians who blame video games for mass shooting (e.g., President Trump's tweet on December 17, 2012: "Video game violence & glorification must be stopped—it is creating monsters!").

However, media violence researchers do *not* make such extreme claims. Instead, mainstream researchers routinely argue that playing violent video games contributes to increasing the odds of behaving aggressively after provocation, mainly by increasing other aggression risk factors, such as anger, hostility, and viewing others as hostile entities (Plante et al., 2020).

Furthermore, video game violence researchers almost always focus on *aggression*, not *violence*. Although aggression and violence are used almost interchangeably in everyday life, they in fact convey two different meanings. In social psychology, aggression is defined as "a behavior that is intended to harm another person who is motivated to avoid that harm" (Allen & Anderson, 2017). In contrast, violence is defined as "an extreme form of aggression that has severe physical harm as its goal" (Bushman & Huesmann, 2010).

From these definitions we see that violence is a subset of physical aggression characterized by extremity, where severe bodily damage or death is the goal. A child pushing his younger sister in anger is an act of aggression, but not violence. A teen shooting a romantic rival is both aggression and violence. Therefore, popular news headlines claiming that "research studies conclude that video games do not cause mass shooting" are inaccurate. The studies do not measure mass shootings—most measure aggression.

Nonetheless, this milder level of aggression is still important, as parents find out when they learn that their children is getting bullied at school, for example. Additionally, having a habitual aggressive behavior problem is one of the largest risk factors for later violence.

Sin 7. Interpretational Errors

Interpretation errors occur when people draw conclusions that are stronger than warranted. A given cross-sectional correlation study may find that violent game play is not associated with aggression. It would be wrong to conclude that violent game play does not *cause* aggression from this one study. Cross-sectional studies can only show whether violent video games and aggression are related, not whether one causes another. Similarly, if violent video game play was found to increase aggression in an ethical experimental study, it would be wrong to conclude that extreme *violence* was caused by video games.

Although a strong correlation between two variables is not strong evidence of causation, it is also true that a lack of correlation is not strong evidence for a lack of causation. As an overly simplistic example, people know from experience that if you skip classes, you will get a worse grade than you could have. However, if people were to graph the correlation between the number of classes missed and grade, you may not see a strong relation, perhaps because too few students in the sample skip classes, or because most students skip at least a few classes.

As seen in figure 2.4, the points—which represent students—are scattered all over the space without a distinct pattern. This does not mean that there is no relation between attendance and grade; it may be that those who skipped classes received extra tutoring, and thus the true relation is being masked. This example illustrates how there could be a causal relationship between two variables even though they are not statistically correlated.

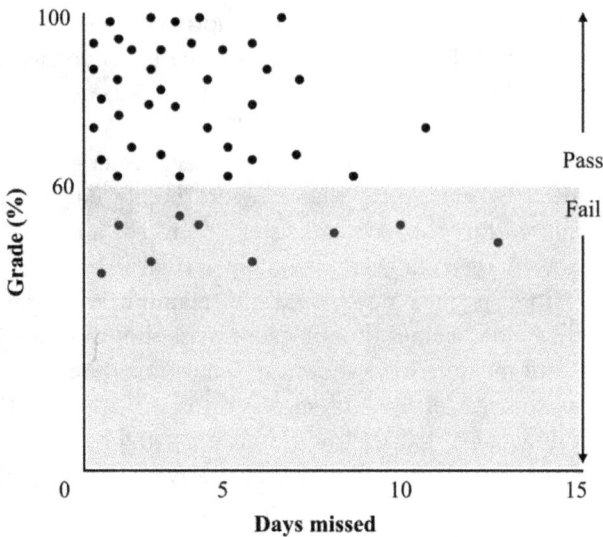

Figure 2.4   The Relationship between Days Missed and Students' Grade.

Furthermore, people could make a mistake by using national data (e.g., population level data) to make sense of the effect of violent video games on children (e.g., individual level data). Some argued that video games are not related to mass shooting, because the United States is the only exceptional country that has both high game sales revenue and violent gun deaths, whereas other countries with high game sales revenue do not have high violent gun deaths (Chang, 2019).

Putting aside the fact that video game researchers do not usually focus on the link between video games and violent crimes, this is an example why it is not appropriate to use the population level data to explain individual level processes. Statistics on violent gun deaths are not very useful in explaining how violent video games may cause physical aggression because violent gun death rates are affected by many other factors, such as regulations on firearms, accessibility of guns, public safety, societal norms, culture, and so on. That is, video games are not the single cause of violent crimes, and violent crimes are not the sole result of video games.

In sum, there are many contributing causes to measures of population level data. Therefore, population level data cannot be used to prove one cause to be false (or true) at the individual level.[6]

Lastly, people make interpretation errors (and exciting news) by overemphasizing single studies, and this seems especially true when a study finds the opposite of what the preponderance of studies demonstrate. "Dog bites man" is not newsworthy, whereas "Man bites dog" is.

As noted throughout the chapter, there are many reasons why a study may obtain a null result. In truth, it is not hard to get a null result. Studies can fail for many more reasons than just those described here. Unfortunately, some critics of video game research focus on studies that find no effect of violent games on aggression, publicizing the "no effect" study as more important, while ignoring the hundreds of studies that do find significant effects.

Such biased interpretation often dampens the significance of well-conducted studies that demonstrate the effect of media violence on children and adolescents, and they miss the point that scientific questions are best answered when considering the preponderance of data, not a few individual studies. Meta-analyses and summaries by independent scientific and public health organizations are therefore very important, because they can weigh the overall effect even while considering the individual studies that find no effects (e.g., American Academy of Pediatrics, Committee on Communication and Media, 2016; American Psychological Association, 2015; Media Violence Commission, International Society for Research on Aggression, 2012).

Why Such Controversies Continue

This chapter has discussed seven reasons why studies can find no effect despite the fact that the preponderance of over six decades of research broadly demonstrates that media violence increases the risk of aggressive, thoughts, feelings, and behaviors.

Despite meta-analytic and public health summaries indicating that media violence exposure is one causal risk factor leading to aggression (e.g., American Academy of Pediatrics, Committee on Communication and Media, 2016; American Academy of Pediatrics, American Psychological Association, American Academy of Child & Adolescent Psychiatry, & American Medical Association, 2000; Anderson et al., 2010; Bushman & Huesmann, 2006; Media Violence Commission, International Society for Research on Aggression, 2012; APA Task Force on Violent Media, 2015; U.S. Surgeon General, 2001), many individuals still argue that there is no consensus on a link between violent video games and aggression.

Why do they continue to make such claims? Psychological processes behind science denial demonstrate many reasons why people cling to disproven beliefs even in the face of strong contrary evidence (Prot & Anderson, 2019).

Research from social psychology shows that people prefer receiving only the information that confirms their own belief, and indeed tend to seek out confirming information. This phenomenon is known as "confirmation bias." By focusing on information that supports their preferred view, people easily disregard evidence that support opposing views. Confirmation bias hinders people from learning about the breadth of evidence that could potentially change their beliefs.

Nonetheless, even after being given clear evidence that their belief is incorrect, people still have an inclination to adhere to their initial beliefs (e.g., Anderson, 2007; Anderson & Lindsay, 1998). They may even feel offended if their belief was proven wrong.

Social psychologist Festinger (1957) used the concept of "cognitive dissonance" to suggest that when people are forced to consider two contradictory thoughts, the contradiction produces discomfort which motivates them to reduce the discomfort. For example, when an important and frequently enacted behavior (e.g., working for a tobacco company or selling violent entertainment products to children) is reported to be harmful (e.g., causing cancer, or harming children), one can reduce the dissonance either by changing the behavior (quitting the tobacco or media company) or dismissing the evidence of harm. It often is easiest to underestimate or dismiss the evidence harm.

Indeed, some people may come to believe that evidence results from a secret scheme created by powerful agencies and figures. By engaging in such conspiratorial thinking, people justify and uphold their preferred beliefs while choosing to neglect contradicting evidence. This kind of belief perseverance contributes to continued denial of science. Note that these are normal psychological processes; those who engage in them are not necessarily mentally unbalanced. In fact, because these processes are so natural it is hard to guard against them, or even to notice when we fall prey to them.

Conclusion

The public controversy on video game violence will likely continue into the future. How can these controversies be resolved? One key to the resolution is scientific literacy. There are many sources of information (mostly from general mass media) that convey inaccurate pictures of media violence research. Do not rely on sensationalized media depictions of violent game research, and do not be lured by catchy news headlines; become a careful reader who can discern facts from opinions.

Furthermore, one should always refer back to the original research findings to understand the actual study results, when possible. Mass media often dramatize study findings to attract people's attention. Often news articles will claim that a study *proved* video games do not cause violence by referring to a questionnaire-based cross-sectional study, which is inherently inaccurate because one thing can still cause another even when they are not statistically correlated, as this chapter has discussed.

In addition, no single study, no matter how well-designed, can "prove" anything in science. People need to examine the full literature, recognizing the strengths and weaknesses inherent in different research designs. Carefully reading the information from the primary source can decrease the alteration of the facts and increases accuracy of the information obtained.

And last, one should not fall into the trap of confirmation bias. Readers of the science studies should open themselves up to various sources of argument from different perspectives. In fact, one should actively seek information that directly challenges their beliefs and biases. Cherry-picking only the evidence that supports one's pre-existing belief just increases the polarization of society, strengthening controversies rather than resolving them. This can happen just as easily with a study that appears to demonstrate an effect as it can with one that appears to show no effect.

Good science relies on being critical and discerning about all studies, and to be willing to re-evaluate your current opinions. Regardless of whether one interprets the collected set of studies as demonstrating an important effect or as an insignificant effect, one must make a fully informed decision after gathering as much data as possible, while bearing in mind the possible "sins" that are frequently committed in media violence research.

Finally, note that we did not say that it is important to hear "both sides" of this debate. That would be another sin—one of the false dilemma, a type of reduction fallacy. Almost every important issue has far more than two sides, and often more than one simple answer. Even calling this issue a "debate" is an error, as it implies two opposing sides of relatively equal validity, and makes a reader assume that they must choose one. The truth is much more nuanced than this, as is the research. You probably shouldn't believe anyone who tells you otherwise.

Notes

1. Random assignment can be done by a coin toss or (more likely) a random number generator. The main reason why experiments allow stronger causal statements than other study types is that *on average* participants in the different experimental conditions will be similar on characteristics (such as gender, socioeconomic background, personality) that might influence the outcome variable,

even for characteristics that are not measured. However, there is no guarantee that the experimental conditions in any specific study are in actuality equal on such characteristics.

2. These same "sins" also occur in some studies that do find harmful effects, which is why the best scholars in this (or any) area of scientific research take quality of studies into account when summarizing the research literature (e.g., Anderson et al., 2010).

3. Of course, such failures of randomization can also work in the other direction, leading a researcher to find a significant effect even when there isn't really a true effect.

4. Actually, one incredible study found a way to do something like this ethically (Dillon & Bushman, 2017). A real handgun was hidden in a room with no ammunition and the firing pin removed. Children came to the study with a best friend or sibling, and were randomly assigned to play a video game (Minecraft), either with guns, swords, or no weapons. Children who played the game with guns or swords (relative to those who played the nonviolent version) handled the gun for much more time, and they more frequently pointed it at their friend or self and pulled the trigger!

5. Actually, when done properly statistically controlling for mediating variables, correlated outcome variables, and correlated predictor variables can be useful, by helping the researcher to test more specific theoretical questions. For example, to test whether aggressive thinking mediates the effect of violent video game exposure on aggressive behavior, one can compare the association between violent game exposure and aggression both without and with aggressive thinking statistically controlled. If this association is larger when aggressive thinking is not controlled, then the data support a mediation hypothesis.

6. This example also demonstrates "sin" 4 – Video game *revenue* is not an appropriate measure of *violent game exposure*. Sales might be more for non-violent games in some countries, for example.

References

AAP Committee on Communications and Media. (2016). Virtual violence. *Pediatrics, 138*(2). https://doi.org/10.1542/peds.2016-1298

Allen, J. J., & Anderson, C. A. (2017). Aggression and violence: Definitions and distinctions. In P. Sturmey (Ed.), *The Wiley handbook of violence and aggression* (pp. 1–14). Hoboken, NJ: Wiley-Blackwell.

American Academy of Pediatrics, American Psychological Association, American Academy of Child & Adolescent Psychiatry, & American Medical Association. (2000, July 26). *Joint statement on the impact of entertainment violence on children.* http://www.aap.org/advocacy/releases/jstmtevc.htm

American Psychological Association. (2015). *Resolution on violent video games.* https://www.apa.org/about/policy/violent-video-games

Anderson, C. A. (2007). Belief perseverance. In R. F. Baumeister & K. D. Vohs (Eds.), *Encyclopedia of social psychology* (pp. 109–110). Thousand Oaks, CA: SAGE.

Anderson, C. A., Berkowitz, L., Donnerstein, E., Huesmann, L. R., Johnson, J., Linz, D., Malamuth, N., & Wartella, E. (2003). The influence of media violence on youth. *Psychological Science in the Public Interest, 4*, 81–110.

Anderson, C. A., Gentile, D. A., & Buckley, K. E. (2007). *Violent video game effects on children and adolescents: Theory, research, and public policy.* New York: Oxford University Press.

Anderson, C. A., & Lindsay, J. J. (1998). The development, perseverance, and change of naive theories. *Social Cognition, 16*, 8–30. https://doi.org/10.1521/soco.1998.16.1.8

Anderson, C. A., Shibuya, A., Ihori, N., Swing, E. L., Bushman, B. J., Sakamoto, A., Rothstein, H. R., & Saleem, M. (2010). Violent video game effects on aggression, empathy, and prosocial behavior in Eastern and Western countries. *Psychological Bulletin, 136*, 151–173.

APA Task Force on Violent Media. (2015). *Technical report on the review of the violent video game literature.*

Bartholow, B. D., & Anderson, C. A. (2002). Effects of violent video games on aggressive behavior: Potential sex differences. *Journal of Experimental Social Psychology, 38*, 283–290.

Bender, J., Rothmund, T., & Gollwitzer, M. (2013). Biased estimation of violent video game effects on aggression: Contributing factors and boundary conditions. *Societies, 3*, 383–398.

Brady, S. S., & Matthews, K. A. (2006). Effects of media violence on health-related outcomes among young men. *Archives of Pediatrics & Adolescent Medicine, 160*(4), 341.

Busching, R., Gentile, D. A., Krahé, B., Möller, I., Khoo, A., Walsh, D. A., & Anderson, C. A. (2015). Testing the reliability and validity of different measures of violent video game use in the United States, Singapore, and Germany. *Psychology of Popular Media Culture, 4*(2), 97–111.

Bushman, B. J., & Huesmann, L. R. (2006). Short-term and long-term effects of violent media on aggression in children and adults. *Archives of Pediatrics & Adolescent Medicine, 160*(4), 348–352.

Bushman, B. J., & Huesmann, L. R. (2010). Aggression. In S. T. Fiske, D. T. Gilbert, & G. Lindzey (Eds.), *Handbook of social psychology* (5th ed., pp. 833–863). Hoboken, NJ: John Wiley & Sons..

Calvert, S. L., Appelbaum, M., Dodge, K. A., Graham, S., Nagayama Hall, G. C., Hamby, S., Fasig-Caldwell, L. G., Citkowicz, M., Galloway, D. P., & Hedges, L. V. (2017). The American Psychological Association task force assessment of violent video games: Science in the service of public interest. *American Psychologist, 72*(2), 126–143.

Chang, A. (2019, August 5). Why video games aren't causing America's gun problem, in one chart. *Vox.* https://www.vox.com/policy-and-politics/2019/8/5/20755092/gun-shooting-video-game-chart

DeLisi, M., Vaughn, M. G., Gentile, D. A., Anderson, C. A., & Shook, J. (2013). Violent video games, delinquency, and youth violence: New evidence. *Youth Violence and Juvenile Justice, 11,* 132–142.

Dillon, K. P., & Bushman, B. J. (2017). Effects of exposure to gun violence in movies on children's interest in real guns. *JAMA Pediatrics, 171*(11), 1057.

Elson, M., Breuer, J., Van Looy, J., Kneer, J., & Quandt, T. (2015). Comparing apples and oranges? Evidence for pace of action as a confound in research on digital games and aggression. *Psychology of Popular Media Culture, 4*(2), 112–125.

Entertainment Software Association. (2019). *Essential facts about games and violence.* https://www.theesa.com/wp-content/uploads/2019/03/EFGamesandViolence.pdf

Exelmans, L., Custers, K., & Van den Bulck, J. (2015). Violent video games and delinquent behavior in adolescents: A risk factor perspective. *Aggressive Behavior, 41*(3), 267–279.

Ferguson, C. J. (2007). The good, the bad and the ugly: A meta-analytic review of positive and negative effects of violent video games. *Psychiatric Quarterly, 78*(4), 309–316. https://doi.org/10.1007/s11126-007-9056-9

Ferguson, C. J. (2019, August 5). Stop blaming video games for mass killings. *The Conversation.* https://theconversation.com/stop-blaming-video-games-for-mass-killings-121472

Festinger, L. (1957). *A theory of cognitive dissonance.* Stanford: Stanford University Press.

Gabbiadini, A., Riva, P., Andrighetto, L., Volpato, C., & Bushman, B. J. (2014). Interactive effect of moral disengagement and violent video games on self-control, cheating, and aggression. *Social Psychological and Personality Science, 5*(4), 451–458.

Gentile, D., Li, D., Khoo, A., Prot, S., & Anderson, C. (2014). Mediators and moderators of long-term violent video game effects on aggressive behavior. *JAMA Pediatrics, 168*(5), 450–457.

Gentile, D. A. (2008). The rating systems for media products. In S. Calvert & B. Wilson (Eds.), *Handbook of children, media, and development* (pp. 527–551). Oxford, England: Blackwell Publishing.

Giancola, P. R., & Parrott, D. J. (2008). Further evidence for the validity of the Taylor aggression paradigm. *Aggressive Behavior, 34,* 214–229.

Hull, J. G., Brunelle, T. J., Prescott, A. T., & Sargent, J. D. (2014). A longitudinal study of risk-glorifying video games and behavioral deviance. *Journal of Personality and Social Psychology, 107*(2), 300–325.

Hyatt, C. S., Chester, D. S., Zeichner, A., & Miller, J. D. (2019). Analytic flexibility in laboratory aggression paradigms: Relations with personality traits vary (slightly) by operationalization of aggression. *Aggressive Behavior, 45*(4), 377–388.

Konijn, E. A., Bijvank, M., & Bushman, B. J. (2007). I wish I were a warrior: The role of wishful identification in the effects of violent video games on aggression in adolescent boys. *Developmental Psychology, 43,* 1038–1044.

Mathur, M. B., & VanderWeele, T. J. (2019). Finding common ground in meta-analysis "wars" on violent video games. *Perspectives on Psychological Science, 14*(4), 705–708. https://doi.org/10.1177/1745691619850104

Media Violence Commission, International Society for Research on Aggression (ISRA). (2012). Report of the media violence commission. *Aggressive Behavior, 38*(5), 335–341.

Möller, I., & Krahé, B. (2009). Exposure to violent video games and aggression in German adolescents: A longitudinal analysis. *Aggressive Behavior, 35*(1), 75–89.

Plante, C., Anderson, C. A., Allen, J. J., Groves, C. L., & Gentile, D. A. (2019). *Game on!: Sensible answers about video games and media violence.* Ames, IA: Zengen LLC.

Prescott, A. T., Sargent, J. D., & Hull, J. G. (2018). Meta-analysis of the relationship between violent video game play and physical aggression over time. *Proceedings of the National Academy of Sciences, 115*(40), 9882–9888.

Prot, S., & Anderson, C. A. (2019). Science denial: Psychological processes underlying denial of science-based medical practices. In A. Lavorgna & A. D. Ronco (Eds.), *Medical misinformation and social harm in non-science based health practices: A multidisciplinary perspective* (pp. 24–37). Abingdon, UK: Routledge.

Przybylski, A. K., & Weinstein, N. (2019). Violent video game engagement is not associated with adolescents' aggressive behaviour: Evidence from a registered report. *Royal Society Open Science, 6*, 171474.

Salmivalli, C. (2010). Bullying and the peer group: A review. *Aggression and Violent Behavior, 15*(2), 112–120.

Siyez, D. M., & Baran, B. (2017). Determining reactive and proactive aggression and empathy levels of middle school students regarding their video game preferences. *Computers in Human Behavior, 72*, 286–295.

Tear, M. J., & Nielsen, M. (2014). Video games and prosocial behavior: A study of the effects of non-violent, violent and ultra-violent gameplay. *Computers in Human Behavior, 41*, 8–13.

Teng, S. K., Chong, G. Y., Siew, A. S., & Skoric, M. M. (2011). Grand theft auto IV comes to Singapore: Effects of repeated exposure to violent video games on aggression. *Cyberpsychology, Behavior, and Social Networking, 14*(10), 597–602.

US Surgeon General. (2001). *Youth violence: A report of the surgeon general* (2001/04/11 ed.). Washington, DC: United States Surgeon General.

Williams, D., & Skoric, M. (2005). Internet fantasy violence: A test of aggression in an online game. *Communication Monographs, 72*, 217–233.

CHAPTER 3

~

Should Internet Addiction and Gaming Addiction Be Categorized as Disorders?

Wayne A. Warburton

Introduction: The Controversy

The first Internet connected mobile phone was launched by Nokia in Finland in 1996, but it wasn't until iPhones became popular in the late 1990s, and the iPad was launched in April 2010, that the use of portable Internet-connected devices started to become widespread. From then a range of such devices proliferated and the take-up was rapid. However, with the capacity to be online 24 hours a day, 7 days a week, at any place with Internet connectivity, came another growing issue.

Psychologists, teachers, school counselors, pediatricians and others who worked with children and adolescents started to report that some children and teens were using screens at a level that was causing significant problems—missing school, stopping other activities, difficulties with offline relationships, substantial sleep deficits, worrying behavioral changes and a constant preoccupation with screen-related activities. There were even reports of screen overuse-related deaths (due to exhaustion, cardiac arrest, and blood clots)[1], and of infants dying from neglect while parents were playing video games.[2]

The notion that some people may be using screens at problematic and even "addictive" levels gained further traction in 2013 when the American Psychiatric Association published the fifth edition of its *Diagnostic and Statistical Manual for Mental Disorders* (DSM-5) and included a new, screen-based disorder in a section for mental health disorders requiring further research. This was termed Internet Gaming Disorder (IGD), with the proposed diagnostic criteria for the disorder being very similar to those for the other DSM "behavioral addiction," Gambling Disorder (i.e., gambling addiction).

This inclusion started a heated controversy. Critics of the decision from the video game industry and the gaming movement, as well as some scholars, claimed that there were insufficient reasons to justify such a disorder being included the *DSM*, and expressed their concerns that a harmless leisure pastime was being pathologized.

The controversy escalated further in late 2017 following a World Health Organization (WHO) proposal to include a similar disorder—Gaming Disorder (GD)—in the 11th edition of its *International Classification of Disease* (*ICD-11*). Despite some very vocal resistance, GD was ratified as a mental health disorder by the WHO in 2019, based on clinical reports and reviews of the growing scientific evidence. The WHO also included a "Hazardous Gaming" diagnosis, which involves video gaming that does not meet criteria for being addiction-like, but *appreciably increases the risk of harmful physical or mental health consequences.*

To date, video game addiction is the only nongambling, screen-based addiction officially classified as a disorder. However, concerns have been raised over the last two decades about other forms of possible "screen addiction" as well. These include internet addiction (IA: also known as Problematic Internet Use or PIU), social media addiction (SMA), smartphone addiction, and pornography addiction. The most researched is IA/PIU, which was first identified as a potential mental health issue by Kimberly Young in the late 1990s.

Adding to the discourse about these screen-based issues, several current and past executives of "tech titans" have provided revelations about the deliberate use of "addictive" design features in their tech products. Alongside these disclosures there has been a trend for the language around screen disorders to shift from discussing "problematic use" to discussing potential for "addiction." Given that substance addiction is already subject to widespread social stigma, it is not hard to see why discussions of screen use in terms of possible addiction have been so controversial.

Other factors have fed into the controversy as well: the vested interests of companies that profit from screen products, or those who benefit from funding from those companies (with these vested interests not always being apparent); the strong feelings of people whose identities strongly align with screen activities such as video gaming; the many benefits of screen use; and the vast majority of people who use screens without issue, among others.

When all these factors are taken into account, it is not surprising that the debate around screen disorders is highly confusing, and even experts in the field have trouble interpreting the research findings and untangling the facts, myths, fictions, and vested interests. This makes it hard to produce a scientifically and clinically grounded perspective, and most attempts to do so face criticism from those who disagree, don't like what is written, or both.

Nevertheless, many parents and professionals who work with children are dealing with issues around problematic or disordered levels of screen use, and finding a perspective that can offer practical assistance is currently a very important undertaking.

In this chapter it will be argued that some people *do* use screens at disordered levels. Clinical experience has revealed young people whose screen use has had consequences for them that can only be described as disastrous: ceasing school attendance altogether from early in middle school; not leaving the bedroom for years on end (literally); chronic sleep deprivation; obesity; serious inactivity-related health problems; loss of relationships and opportunities; aggression and violence when others try to limit screen use; and a sense of having no personal worth or prospects offline, with associated depression and anxiety.

For this reason, a case will be made that it is important to officially recognize screen-based addictions such as IGD and GD as clinical disorders.[3] This will allow parents and professionals to ascertain when there really is a problem, much in the same way that we determine when normal eating becomes disordered (i.e., anorexia or bulimia), or when sadness becomes clinical depression. This will also provide a basis for providing appropriate assistance to those who need it, without stigmatizing the vast majority of users who have no such problems.

However, before looking at how to detect and manage screen-based disorders, it may be helpful to first look at the research findings around behavioral addictions generally and screen-based addictions specifically.

Behavioral Addictions

Reward and Addiction in the Brain

The human reward system is complex, and a full description of its operation, including in addiction, is beyond the scope of this chapter. However, an understanding of the key principles may be helpful in understanding screen-based addictions.

Humans are motivated to undertake behaviors that ensure their survival and the survival of the species (eating, sex, etc.), and this motivation often originates in the brain's reward system.

Such behaviors release a neurotransmitter (brain chemical) called dopamine, which is produced by a relatively small number of neurons in two tiny areas of the brain, and is distributed through pathways to parts of the brain related to pleasure, reward, and goal-directed behavior. Dopamine causes us to feel pleasure when released in a part of the brain called the nucleus accumbens, and motivates us to seek more of whatever caused its release. So, if we do something, *and* dopamine is released, *and* it gives us pleasure, then we will be motivated to do that thing more.

Crucially, there are brakes on the system so we don't eat, or have sex, or seek pleasure to the point of death. Dopamine is produced most *in anticipation* of something rewarding, and especially when we are unsure when that reward will come. Once we have the reward, two other neurotransmitters, serotonin and GABA, are also released. Serotonin reduces arousal and creates a sense of contentment and satisfaction, while GABA opposes the effect of dopamine. These processes put a brake on the reward process.

However, the braking system does not always work. There are several theories as to why, but some failures may involve increases in the "transcription factor" Delta FosB. Dopamine release produces an increase in Delta FosB, which accumulates over time. At a certain level, which is different for different people, Delta FosB motivates people to compulsively seek substances or experiences that release dopamine, and does so for several months after the initial dopamine triggers are gone, setting up a pattern of craving in their absence. Such cravings are a key part of addiction.

Addiction becomes more likely when something that triggers dopamine keeps promising a reward that comes randomly or infrequently, and gives a reward that doesn't fully satisfy the person. This process may trigger dopamine so regularly that the point is reached where high Delta FosB levels create a compulsion for that thing. At this point, people might be motivated to seek or do that thing even when it brings little or no pleasure and comes at a personal cost.

Can People Become Addicted to a Behavior?

In the 1990s, the law, medicine, and most professions treated problem gambling simply as a failure of restraint and/or morality rather than as an addiction. This is no longer true. Gambling Disorder is now widely accepted as a psychiatric disorder of addiction.

In the fifth revision of the *DSM* (2013), pathological gambling was re-termed *Disordered Gambling*, removed from the impulse control disorders section, and re-categorized with the "Substance-related and addictive disorders" (i.e., with substance addictions). Similarly, in 2019, *Gambling Disorder* was included in the "Substance use and related disorders" chapter of the 11th revision of the *ICD*.

These changes follow research showing that (a) the impact of gambling on the brain function and reward systems of gambling addicts is comparable to the impacts of addictive substances on the brains of substance addicts (e.g., see Grant et al., 2010), and (b) that gambling disordered individuals exhibit the same key behaviors we see in other addictions: craving, impaired control over use, and continued use despite serious adverse consequences.

Although some scholars still question whether behavioral addictions are possible, it is increasingly hard to support this viewpoint in the face of the large body of evidence that disordered gambling is a form of behavioral addiction.

Such skepticism is also at odds with the revised definition of addiction adopted by the American Society for Addiction Medicine (ASAM) in 2011,[4] as a *chronic disease of brain reward, motivation, memory and related circuitry* that can be rooted in either substances or behaviors. In their explanatory document, ASAM noted that addiction is about *what happens in a person's brain when they are exposed to rewarding substances or rewarding behaviors, and it is more about reward circuitry in the brain and related brain structures than it is about the external chemicals or behavior that 'turn on' that reward circuitry.*

Despite the now widespread clinical acceptance of behavioral addictions such as gambling disorder, some critics of the notion of screen-based addictions still suggest that such an addiction cannot be compared to a drug addiction.

They note, for example, that there is a limit on the level of dopamine release that can occur naturally within the brain, and that the dopamine release from behaviors like screen use must occur within this limited range. Addictive substances on the other hand, can artificially increase dopamine up to 10 times the natural levels, thus having a much greater effect on the brain reward circuitry, and, by this argument, making drugs addictive in a way that behaviors cannot be.

Although this argument sounds convincing at face value, the more relevant question is this: *how much* dopamine increase is needed to cause the changes in the brain that underlie true addiction? The extreme level of addiction found in some gambling disordered individuals (e.g., wearing diapers to avoid leaving a slot machine to go to the toilet, committing theft and fraud to fund gambling, and persistence despite huge personal costs) shows us that dopamine increases within the natural limit are clearly sufficient to cause a severe addiction.

Screen-Based Addictions

Are Online Platforms and Products Designed to Be Addictive?

Tristan Harris, ex-design ethicist at Google, Marc Benioff, CEO of cloud computing company Salesforce, and ex-Facebook President Sean Parker are

among a number of senior "tech titan" executives who have recently explic-
itly stated that many tech products are designed to hook or addict users, and
do so by exploiting user vulnerabilities.

The reason is simple: all commercial online products that are free to
users rely on advertising and/or in-app purchases to make money, and the
more minutes that users spend in front of a screen using that product, the
greater the revenue. Thus, to be financially viable in a competitive and
crowded marketplace, an online product must keep users at the screen as
long as the products of competitors or longer than the products of competitors. If competitors are using "addictive" technology, then this becomes the
standard.

The art of creating online products with addictive potential has been
termed *persuasive design* or *persuasive technology*, and focuses on several key
principles—motivating people to use the product by tapping in to their vulnerabilities (e.g., key needs such as the need to feel socially accepted), making the product easy to use, fostering a feeling of investment, and including
as many features as possible that keep the person at the screen.

In terms of taking advantage of user vulnerabilities, a key feature of many
online products with addictive potential is the use of advanced artificial
intelligences (AIs) that monitor users in real time, use a wide range of return
data to ascertain periods of specific vulnerability for each user, and tailor
the experience of that user accordingly. For example, relevant advertisements may be shown just when the person is identified as feeling worthless
or lonely, or targeted prompts may appear when it seems the user is losing
interest.

Such practices by a major social media platform were reported by journalists from *The Australian* in 2018, and have been confirmed by ex-industry
executives like Sean Parker.

Persuasive design services have been made commercially available
through companies such as Dopamine Labs (later re-branded to Boundless
Mind), and may use various methods (persuasive design techniques, neuroscience, AI services) to optimize the way that apps modify human behavior.

In terms of keeping people at the screen there are numerous devices used:
notifications, banners, prompts, reminders and autoplay (among others).
In video games there are further features, such as not being able to save
between levels, games and teams evolving when the player is absent, less
reward for short periods of play and features that slow down play.

Immersion in the virtual world also causes the person to be more drawn
to the screen and less aware of the offline world. This phenomenon is widely
used in establishments with gambling machines, where the rooms are darker

and there are rarely any windows, television screens, or other reminders of the outside world to distract the gambler.

In addition, because dopamine levels are particularly raised in anticipation of a reward and reduce once the person feels satisfied, designers create products that never quite reach a conclusion, and have rewards that are intermittent, unpredictable and not fully satisfying. Coupled with intermittent reward schedules (e.g., likes, in-game rewards, loot boxes), reward loops, and design features that make the user keep wanting more (such as small wins and near misses), this creates a consistent anticipation that something rewarding is coming, with an associated dopamine release.

However, because these products are also designed to avoid the user feeling fully satisfied, there is less opportunity for the processes that put the brake on reward seeking. This may facilitate addiction in some people.

Together, these deliberate design features clearly enhance the ability of many online products to keep the user at the screen, and seem to do so using methods that may cause some users to become addicted, as is the case with gambling machines.

Clinical Evidence for Screen Addictions

Prevalence. Although prevalence estimates have varied, probably due to the use of multiple definitions and diverse measures, earlier studies have tended to find problematic levels of screen use at around 5–10% across countries and regions (e.g., Tam & Walter, 2013), although there has been considerable variance.

Since the advent of the IGD and then GD diagnoses, the emphasis of prevalence studies has shifted more to disordered levels of video game use, and the use of instruments that specifically target their diagnostic criteria. In more recent population-based studies, rates of IGD in youth have tended to average around 2%, with higher rates in Asian countries and lower rates in European countries (e.g., Paulus et al., 2018). However, further work is needed to establish a single standardized measure that can be used to reliably identify video game use at a disordered/addictive level, and empirically establish prevalence rates.

Screen addiction and the brain. In terms of impacts on the brain, numerous studies show that the human brain is plastic, and can change in structure and function according to how the person uses it (think London taxi drivers, who need to memorize large amounts of map information and have been found to have an enlarged hippocampus, a key memory region). Generally, the "use it or lose it" maxim applies to the brain, with activities that challenge thinking linked with increased neural connectivity, and inactivity linked with atrophy (loss of gray matter and neural connections).

Early brain imaging studies tended to focus on internet addiction or early measures of online gaming addiction, and often compared a sample of 15–20 participants who met criteria for addiction with a similar number of matched healthy controls. Later studies used larger samples and more targeted measures that closely conformed to the DSM-5 proposed IGD diagnostic criteria. Although these studies have looked at various areas of brain function, the results are generally consistent and reveal structural and functional differences (on average) between the addicted participants and non-addicted controls.

These include (a) atrophy in various parts of the cortex, including regions linked to higher functions such as the prefrontal cortex, (b) reduced cortical thickness (including in the frontal lobe), (c) altered white matter integrity and density, (d) impairment on cognitive tasks, and (e) changes to function in the brain reward systems consistent with addiction (see Pontes et al., 2017; Yao et al., 2017 for reviews).

Together, the brain imaging findings seem to suggest two things. First, there seems to be a clinical, neurological difference between screen-addicted individuals and the normal population (e.g., Kuss et al., 2018), with some of those brain differences consistent with addiction. Second, these findings are similar for both internet addiction and video gaming addiction. This suggests that internet addiction may be a genuine addictive disorder.

Case studies. Disordered screen use is also evident in the growing number of published case studies related to disordered video gaming (and also internet addiction). Although each gaming case is different, there are a number of frequently found commonalities involving features that are consistent with addiction: increasing time gaming and thinking about gaming, playing at times of stress, becoming irritable, upset and sometimes aggressive/violent when unable to play, and continuing to play despite substantial negative consequences.

Usually there is also a marked reduction in time spent studying or working, undertaking other activities, and relating to family and friends offline. In addition, case studies often report corresponding declines in mental health—most notably depression and various forms of anxiety. Some case studies document instances of disordered screen use at extreme levels and provide compelling evidence that such individuals require substantial clinical intervention.

Reviews and meta-analyses. There are now numerous well-conducted and systematic reviews of the growing literature on IGD, as well as some reviews of IA/PIU (e.g., Paulus et al., 2018). Although a full analysis is not possible here, these reviews typically find that (a) a subgroup of screen users show symptoms consistent with addiction, but (b) fully understanding this group is hampered by disagreement around diagnostic criteria, lack of standardized measurement instruments and a lack of longitudinal and long-term follow up studies.

Comorbidity. One issue raised by critics of screen disorder diagnoses is that many who meet criteria also have other mental health problems. For this reason, they suggest that disorders like IGD and GD may not be standalone disorders but merely symptomatic of other mental health issues.

It is certainly true that among those with such diagnoses there are often co-morbid issues such as Autism Spectrum Disorder, ADHD and depression (among others). However, co-morbidity doesn't preclude a standalone diagnosis. Indeed, in mental health "pure" disorders are the exception rather than the rule. To give one example, more than 50% of gambling disordered individuals have issues such as depression, anxiety, post-traumatic stress, and substance addiction that preceded or coexist with their gambling disorder, and yet there is no longer a debate as to whether this is a standalone mental health disorder.

Isn't this simply a taste of the future? Some people have suggested that the future is digital, that most future communication will be digital, and that constant screen use is really the new "normal," not some form of disorder. Thus, goes the argument, people who try to suggest IGD/GD and IA are disorders are really engaging in a "moral panic" about something that is in reality just normal behavior in a digital world.

The key weakness of this argument is that it ignores basic biology. While the future will involve a lot of digital engagement, humans *need* face-to-face and physical contact for their health. Such contact releases important hormones (such as oxytocin) and supports a healthy immune system. When people do not get enough physical and face-to-face contact their immune system becomes compromised and they become prone to developing autoimmune and inflammatory diseases, as well as to later cognitive decline. Their life expectancy also drops (see Sigman, 2009).

In terms of psychology, children need face-to-face play and interaction for normal development—online interaction does *not* have the same developmental benefits as face-to-face interaction.

Thus, for both developmental and biological reasons, digital interaction needs to be interleaved with face-to-face interaction for a person to be healthy, even in the digital age.

Evidence overall. The study of screen-based disorders is in its infancy, and getting a complete picture is hampered by a lack of consensus on diagnostic criteria, the use of multiple measures, and little research following the pathway to addiction over time. However the convergence of brain imaging evidence and clinical evidence seems sufficient to assert that there are clearly some individuals whose screen use is at disordered levels, and that the disorder has the key hallmarks of addiction for some of those individuals.

Solutions

Symptoms, Risk Factors and Early Warning Signs

It is important for parents and professionals who are concerned that their child or client has IGD/GD or another screen-based addiction to understand the risk factors, early warning signs and symptoms of a disorder.

The diagnostic criteria for IGD and GD are shown below. The *DSM-5* IGD criteria are linked more closely to known characteristics of addiction (e.g., preoccupation, tolerance, withdrawal, deceit about use, difficulty stopping, continuance despite serious negative consequences and so on). The *ICD-11* criteria are a little more general and offer the user more latitude to take into account issues and dysfunctions not specifically noted in the *DSM*.

While there are no official criteria for other screen-based disorders such as IA/PIU, SMA, smartphone addiction, and pornography addiction, an argument could be made that a similar pattern of dysfunction related to use of these screen media could also be treated as indicative of a potential disorder (that is, the person has similar symptoms to IGD/GD, but the symptoms are related to internet use, social media use etc., rather than to video game use).

For screen use disorders it is also important to get a sense of the *severity* of the problem: children/teens who are at risk of developing a problem, versus those who actually have a problem, versus those whose problem is at an addiction level that requires substantive intervention.

Generally speaking, children/teens *at risk* will have more of the risk characteristics noted below and tick some boxes for diagnostic criteria; children/teens with *problematic/hazardous levels of use* will tick more diagnostic boxes and have a substantial impairment in at least one important area of life (school, relationships, mental health etc.); and those *with a disorder/addiction* will show a number of symptoms at a high level of severity and with substantial impairment.

DSM-5—*Proposed Criteria for Diagnosing IGD*

Persistent and recurrent use of the Internet to engage in games, often with other players, leading to *clinically significant impairment or distress*. Key criteria are:

1. preoccupation with internet games;
2. withdrawal symptoms when internet gaming is taken away (may be indicated by irritability, anxiety, or sadness);

3. tolerance, resulting in the need to spend increasing amounts of time engaged in internet games;
4. unsuccessful attempts to control participation in internet games;
5. loss of interests in previous hobbies and entertainment as a result of, and with the exception of, internet games;
6. continued excessive use of internet games despite knowledge of psychosocial problems;
7. deceiving family members, therapists, or others regarding the amount of internet gaming;
8. use of internet games to escape or relieve a negative or dysphoric mood (e.g. feelings of helplessness, guilt, anxiety, stress, worries); and
9. jeopardizing or losing a significant relationship, job, or education or career opportunity because of participation in internet games.

A diagnosis of IGD would require experiencing five or more of these symptoms within a year.

ICD-11—*Criteria for Diagnosing GD*
GD is defined as a pattern of gaming behavior ("digital-gaming" or "video-gaming") characterized by:

- impaired control over gaming;
- increasing priority given to gaming over other activities to the extent that gaming takes precedence over other interests and daily activities; and
- continuation or escalation of gaming despite the occurrence of negative consequences.

For GD to be diagnosed, the behavior pattern must be of *sufficient severity to result in significant impairment* in personal, family, social, educational, occupational or other important areas of functioning.

Symptoms would normally have been evident for at least 12 months.

Risk Factors for GDs
The profile of an individual at-risk for a screen addiction is yet to be fully settled, but there are some commonly reported factors that seem to increase the risk (e.g., Sugaya et al., 2019). These include a high level of impulsiveness and risk taking, boredom-proneness, various key needs not being met in off-screen life (e.g., belonging/social inclusion, self-esteem, control, mastery), a family environment lacking in cohesion and warmth, pre-existing disorders such as AD/ADHD, low parental control over screen use, and problems with peers.

Recent research in Australia suggests that the combination of impulsivity/ low self-control and low offline need satisfaction may be a potent predictor of IGD risk (Warburton, Parkes & Sweller).

Early Warning Signs
There is no definitive list, but some things commonly seen are an increase in video game use and/or time online, combined with:

- An increase in talk about video games, gaming, and other gamers;
- More time spent in the bedroom, often to play video games, or be online;
- Getting up early to play video games or go online (sometimes setting an alarm to go online before the rest of the family is awake);
- Becoming increasingly tired and irritable;
- Tantrums/aggression when asked to stop playing a game or go offline;
- Withdrawing from other activities to spend more time online or gaming;
- Lying about time spent online;
- Noticeable declines in key areas (e.g., worse school grades, less offline time with friends/family, less participation in normal activities including physical activity).

Prevention
It is easier to prevent an addiction than to treat one, and the basic principle that potential addictive problems should be addressed sooner rather than later is important. The key is to know the risk factors and early warning signs, and, if you think there is a potential problem, to work with the child toward establishing patterns of healthy use.

My own view is that a healthy media diet is like a healthy food diet—look for *moderation* in amount, *more of the good stuff* (educational, prosocial, positive media) and *less of the unhelpful stuff* (violent, antisocial, mind numbing media), and *have regard to the consumer's age* (Warburton, 2012). It is hard to go wrong with a media diet based on these principles. Here are some practical ways to work toward a healthy media diet and manage issues around increasing screen use:

- *Talk.* Often kids/teens aren't aware of the developmental importance of using digital media in a healthy way or of getting enough sleep, so having a conversation about a healthy lifestyle that includes balanced screen use as well as healthy food use and sufficient sleep and exercise can be helpful.

- *Plan*. Part of this conversation can be setting up a Family Media Plan (go to https://www.healthychildren.org/English/media/Pages/default.aspx). This involves sitting down as a family and agreeing on limits and rules around media use.
- *Devices*. Keep all screens out of the bedroom at night (maybe into a device basket or charging station) and encourage screen use in public areas rather than hidden in the bedroom.
- *Monitor*. A large longitudinal study found that the more parents monitored their children's screen use, the better the child's grades, sleep and prosocial behavior, and the lower their body mass index (BMI) and aggression. Monitoring is best if it includes being actively involved with children's media use rather than simply having a passive knowledge of what they are doing.
- *Content*. Aim for more of the good stuff, less of the unhelpful stuff.
- *Balance*. Look for a balance between physical activity and online activity, aiming for more physical activity than screen time. Balance screen time with "green time."
- *Posture:* Workplaces are increasingly concerned with muscular-skeletal issues that arise from screen use (which is repetitive and sedentary), and the same applies for recreational use. Reducing repetition and having regular breaks to move around are both important.
- *Sleep*. Sleep is crucial for healthy development, and establishing regular sleep-time routines, using beds only for sleep, and putting as much time as possible between sleep and screen use (which releases arousing neurochemicals), are all important strategies.
- *Needs*. Children, teens, and young adults who develop screen addictions often tend to have unmet needs offline. If you are worried about someone who is showing some early warning signs of problematic screen use, look for needs that the screen might meet that are not being met in real life, and then try to address the underlying problem. For example, a socially isolated kid with low self-esteem and few skills will be drawn less to the online world if they have offline friends, develop some new offline skills and start to feel good about themselves for having those skills.
- *Self-control*. Difficulties with "executive functions" such as impulsivity, risk taking, and self-control are risk factors for screen-based problems. A child with these issues often benefits from specifically designed executive function strategies, exercises, and therapy. There are various online resources, and psychologists and other therapists can also help.

Treatment

If an individual has a screen disorder, or problematic levels of use, there are various group-based and individual treatment regimes that can be used, often with success. Describing those treatments in detail is beyond the scope of this chapter, but it is helpful to have some sense of what is out there.

Most regimes use a combination of therapeutic approaches, including cognitive behavioral therapy (CBT: changing unhelpful patterns of thinking), motivational interviewing (MI: helping the person come to the point of wanting to make positive changes in their life), family therapy (working with the family unit to reduce things the family does that support screen addiction and replace them with things that support healthy use), counseling, and peer support groups (among others).

These psychological therapies are sometimes combined with drug-based therapies, with various antidepressant drugs being used with some success for both IGD and IA clients. There has also been some success using anti-anxiety medications, and one treatment regime for IA was more successful when an electroacupuncture component was added (see King et al., 2017; Kuss & Fernando-Lopez, 2016 for reviews). There is evidence for the effectiveness of both group-based and one-on-one therapy.

When considering treatments, it is important to keep in mind that the recognition of IGD and GD as disorders is quite recent. Most mental health disorders have a long history of researchers and clinicians carefully testing and refining both the diagnostic criteria and treatments. For IGD and GD this process is in the early stages, with more research needed. In particular we need well-designed, properly controlled clinical trials (see King et al., 2017) as well as the testing and refinement of diagnostic criteria and measures.

It is crucial to note, though, that this does *not mean* the disorders are not real, or that treatments are ineffective, or that we should not treat screen disorders until the knowledge base grows. In the past it would have been unconscionable to refuse treatment to clinically depressed and suicidal clients simply because the diagnostic criteria and treatments were still being refined, and the same principles apply to screen-based disorders. Those with very disordered use need immediate assistance. In any case, the available evidence suggests that many treatments are quite successful, with clients often making substantial progress within three–six months, as evidenced by symptoms decreasing and key functions returning toward normal.

Conclusions

Based on research and clinical reports, it seems clear that screen use can become disordered for some people, and that in extreme cases this looks similar to other addictions both clinically and in the brain. Although only IGD and GD are currently officially ratified as mental health disorders, a substantial body of research seems to suggest that other forms of disordered screen use, including internet addiction, may also exist.

Although the case for these conclusions seems to be strong, the controversy around screen addiction is likely to continue for some time yet. However, it is crucial that one consideration rises above the "debate": there is a group of people whose lives are severely disrupted by their patterns of screen use. These people need help, and in a civil society should be able to receive it.

Notes

1. McCrum, K. (2015, September 3). *Tragic teen gamer dies after 'playing computer for 22 days in a row.* Mirror, UK. https://www.mirror.co.uk/news/world-news/tragic-te en-gamer-dies-after-6373887

2. Salmon, A. (2010, April 2). Couple: Internet gaming addiction led to baby's death. *CNN News.* http://edition.cnn.com/2010/WORLD/asiapcf/04/01/korea.p arents.starved.baby/index.html

3. See also Warburton and Tam (2019).

4. Both the *Definition of addiction* and *Definition of addiction: Frequently asked questions* documents are available from ASAM at: https://www.asam.org

Bibliography

Grant, J. E., Potenza, M. N., Weinstein, A., & Gorelick, D. D. (2010). Introduction to behavioral addictions. *American Journal of Drug and Alcohol Abuse, 36*(5), 233–241. https://doi.org/10.3109/00952990.2010.491884

King, D. L., Delfabbro, P. H., Wu, A. M. S., Doh, Y. Y., Kuss, D. J., Pallesen, S., Mentzoni, R., Carragher, N., & Sakuma, H. (2017). Treatment of Internet gaming disorder: An international systematic review and CONSORT evaluation. *Clinical Psychology Review, 54,* 123–133. https://doi.org/10.1016/j.cpr.2017.04.002

Kuss, D. J., & Lopez-Fernandez, O. (2016). Internet addiction and problematic Internet use: A systematic review of clinical research. *World Journal of Psychiatry, 6*(1), 143–176. https://doi.org/10.5498/wjp.v6.i1.143

Kuss, D. J., Pontes, H. M., & Griffiths, M. D. (2018). Neurobiological correlates in Internet gaming disorder: A systematic literature review. *Frontiers in Psychiatry, 9,* 166. https://doi.org/10.3389/fpsyt.2018.00166

Paulus, F. W., Ohmann, S., von Gontardi, A., & Popow, C. (2018). Internet gaming disorder in children and adolescents: A systematic review. *Developmental Medicine and Child Neurology, 60*(7), 645–659. https://doi.org/10.1111/dmcn.13754

Pontes, H. M., Kuss, D. J., & Griffiths, M. D. (2017). Psychometric assessment of Internet gaming disorder in neuroimaging studies: A systematic review. In C.

Montag & M. Reuter (Eds.), *Internet addiction, studies in neuroscience, psychology and behavioral economics* (pp. 181–208). Springer: Cham. https://doi.org/10.1007/9 78-3-319-46276-9_11

Sigman, A. (2009). Well connected? The biological implications of 'social networking'. *Biologist, 56*(1), 14–20.

Sugaya, N., Shirasaka, T., Takahashi, K., & Kanda, H. (2019). Bio-psychosocial factors of children and adolescents with internet gaming disorder: A systematic review. *BioPsychoSocial Medicine, 13*, 3. https://doi.org/10.1186/s13030-019-0144-5

Tam, P., & Walter, G. (2013). Problematic internet use in childhood and youth: Evolution of a 21st century affliction. *Australasian Psychiatry, 21*, 533–536. https://doi.org/10.1177/1039856213509911

Warburton, W. A. (2012). Growing up fast and furious in a media saturated world. In W. A. Warburton & D. Braunstein (Eds.), *Growing up fast and furious: Reviewing the impacts of violent and sexualised media on children* (pp. 1–33). Sydney: The Federation Press.

Warburton, W. A., Parkes, S., & Sweller, N. (under review). Internet gaming disorder: Evidence for a risk and resilience approach. *Australian and New Zealand Journal of Psychiatry.*

Warburton, W. A., & Tam, P. (2019). *Untangling the weird, wired web of gaming disorder and its classification.* HealthEd Expert Monograph 43. Sydney: HealthEd.

Yao, Y., Liu, L., Ma, S., Shi, X., Zhou, N., Zhang, J., & Potenza, M. N. (2017). Functional and structural neural alterations in Internet gaming disorder: A systematic review and meta-analysis. *Neuroscience and Biobehavioral Reviews, 83*, 313–324. http://dx.doi.org/10.1016/j.neubiorev.2017.10.029

CHAPTER 4

~

Does Pornography Affect Teenagers?
Paul J. Wright

Introduction

Heated debates about whether the use of pornography (i.e., media content depicting nudity and explicit sexual acts designed to arouse the viewer) is helpful, harmful, or inconsequential have been part of social discourse in the United States and many other countries for decades. Given policies attempting to limit the use of pornography to adults, as well as sensitivities about conducting sex research with teenage samples, research on older users was predominate for many years. Research on pornography and teenagers has now become quite common, however, for two reasons. First, the proliferation of easily accessible pornography online rendered unsustainable any lingering notions about the content being exclusively "adults only." Second, there has been an increased acceptance of the research community's position that it is better to study and understand teenage behaviors that are going to happen anyway than to look the other way and remain unaware of problems and potential evidence-based solutions.

The purpose of this chapter is to provide an up-to-date summary of research on controversial questions about teenagers' use of pornography and how it might problematically impact them. Questions about the effects of pornography on teenagers are controversial on two levels. The first and primary level is the question of impact—there has been disagreement about whether there are any problematic effects, and if so, their degree of conse-quence. The second level concerns the definition of "problematic." A par-ticular lesson about sex imparted by pornography may be seen as prosocial by one person and antisocial by another, for example. This second-level controversy must be acknowledged and taken seriously. But it is not the focus of the present work.

This chapter focuses (a) on the question of the direction and magnitude of effects that have generally been identified in the scholarly literature as problematic and (b) research on potential remediating mechanisms. Research on samples aged 17 years and younger is prioritized. When research with teenagers is scarce or nonexistent, findings from adults are utilized but caveated as such.

Controversy I: Do Teenagers Learn Problematic Lessons about Sex and Self from Pornography?

Pornography Use among Teenagers

As is the case with any media genre, exposure is a prerequisite for pedagogical potential. It is common to find reports of pornography use in studies of teenagers both nationally and internationally. Studies documenting teenage pornography use have been carried out in the United States, China, Israel, the Netherlands, the Czech Republic, the United Kingdom, Belgium, Sweden, Italy, and Korea, among others. As a specific illustration, a representative study of teenagers aged 16–19 conducted in Australia found that 93% of boys and 72% of girls had seen pornography in the past year (Rissel et al., 2017). Certainly, there is variation in the degree and intensity of teenagers' use of pornography. But that some exposure has become normative for many adolescents is a consistent finding across studies.

Problematic Messages about Sex and Self in Pornography

Sex researchers define sexual scripts as perceptual, attitudinal, and behavioral lessons about appropriate, normative, and rewarding sexuality that human beings learn both directly and inferentially from observing the sexual behavior of others. Content analyses of sexual behaviors depicted in pornography have led to concern about the messages pornography sends teenagers in five particular areas: aggression, sexual risk, gender, impersonal sex, and body image.

Disagreement about the prevalence of aggression in pornography is one of the oldest controversies in this area of study. Several factors have prevented scholarly consensus, but the primary factor has been definitional. If aggression is defined as overt, forced, and unambiguously nonconsensual sex, then it is clear that aggression is rare in the pornography consumed by the average user (although this type of content exists and can be found accidentally or intentionally if desired by a particular viewer). Conversely, if aggression is defined more broadly as physical or verbal acts generally associated with harmful intent and impact where there is a clear perpetrator and target, aggression is not uncommon in popular pornography.

As illustration, a content analysis of popular pornographic videos found that 88% of scenes contained some form of physical aggression and 49% of scenes showed some form of verbal aggression (Bridges et al., 2010). Studies suggest that the most common forms of physical aggression are spanking, gagging, hair pulling, and choking. Other forms of physical aggression that have been observed include pushing, kicking, biting, slapping, use of weapons, whipping, pinching, and smothering. Studies suggest that name-calling is the most common form of verbal aggression. Regardless of whether the aggression is physical or verbal, men are more likely to be the perpetrators and women the targets. Teenage actresses are just as likely to be aggressed against as older actresses (Shor, 2019).

The risk of an unintended pregnancy or sexually transmitted infection (STI) increases substantially when sex occurs without condoms. For this reason, communication and public health researchers have increasingly analyzed pornography for its presentation of unprotected sex. Results indicate that condomless sex is the norm (although it should be noted that pornography featuring men having sex with men is more likely than opposite sex pornography to depict protected sex). Pornography featuring teenagers is no exception to this rule. For instance, a content analysis of 50 pornographic videos featuring male-female interactions with teenage girls found that only one video depicted condom use (Vannier et al., 2014).

Gendered depictions have also been a concern. Principally, analysts have investigated the concern that pornography depicts power imbalances between men and women and sends the message that women are sexual objects. The "male perpetrator-female target" dynamic mentioned previously in the discussion of aggression speaks directly to the commonality of gendered power imbalances in popular pornography. But other findings are also indicative of power imbalances that favor men. Studies of videos and websites have found, for example, that men were cast as supervisors, business people, or other professionals while women were cast as students, clerical staff, and housewives. An important study on the question of objectification was recently conducted by Fritz and Paul (2017). Employing a comprehensive range of indicators (e.g., stripping, excessive focus on genitals), this study of one of the most popular free-pornography websites found that women were significantly more likely to be objectified than men in the content consumed by the typical user (i.e., mainstream content).

Because many parents encourage their children to adopt a relational rather than an instrumental view of sex, there has also been trepidation that pornography presents sex as an impersonal act. Sex is impersonal when devotion, tenderness, and faithfulness are either not present or not valued. Unlike the question of aggression, there is consensus among scholars that pornography's approach to sex is highly impersonal. Peter and Valkenburg (2006) observe, for example, that pornography "presents sex as a merely physical, self-indulgent activity between casual, uncommitted partners" (p. 640).

Finally, as adults have become more cognizant of the fact that many youth struggle with body-image issues, scholars have responded to the assertion that both male and female actors in pornography oftentimes have idealized and unrealizable physical features (e.g., extraordinary penile length and girth for men, large and perky breasts for women). Although the physical features of pornographic performers have not received as much formal content analytic attention as the previous categories, the writings of scholars who have studied pornography suggest that many actors and actresses do have enviable physical attributes that might lead young viewers to feel inadequate (Tylka, 2015).

Research on Pornography and Teenage Sexual Socialization

Definitively establishing cause and effect relationships for any aspect of human thought or behavior is challenging, and the area of pornography's socializing effects on teenagers is no exception. The gold-standard for causal evidence, the randomized control/treatment group experimental method, is unavailable, as for ethical and/or legal reasons researchers have not assigned some teenagers to view pornography, others not to, and then observed the results. In lieu of the experimental method, researchers have surveyed teenagers about their use of pornography and various sexual beliefs, attitudes, and behaviors. Embedded within these surveys have been other questions that might explain why correlations between pornography use and a particular area of sexuality might be falsely interpreted as causal.

For example, rather than pornography causing teenagers to be more accepting of casual sex, lower levels of religiousness may lead some youth to be more likely to view pornography and also be more positive toward uncommitted sexual explorations. By measuring and including in analyses these types of alternative explanations, confidence grows that any pornography-sexuality correlations are in fact due to sociosexual learning. Also, as causes must precede their effects in time, scholars are increasingly using longitudinal panel designs to study how pornography might affect teenagers' views of sex and self. In a longitudinal panel design, data are gathered from the same participants on more than one occasion, making it possible to address the question of the time-order of relationships between variables (i.e., does pornography use now predict some aspect of teenage sexuality later?). Finally, in recent years, there has been an increase in a methodological technique called meta-analysis, where scholars statistically aggregate results across all of the available literature. This section briefly synopsizes research findings using these methods in the areas of aggression, sexual risk, gender, impersonal sex, and body image.

Wright et al. (2016) meta-analyzed the findings of five studies of the association between pornography use and teenagers' sexually aggressive behavior (e.g., sexual coercion, sexual harassment). Results indicated an association of medium strength between the two variables, such that the more pornography teenagers consumed, the more likely they were to be sexually aggressive. Three of these studies were longitudinal. In each of the longitudinal studies, pornography consumption at an earlier time point was correlated with sexual aggression at a later time point.

Tokunaga et al. (2020) meta-analyzed the findings of six studies of the association between pornography use and teenagers' engagement in condomless sex. Results indicated a small association between the two variables, with higher levels of pornography use correlating with a higher likelihood of having condomless sex. Five of the six studies in this analysis were longitudinal.

No meta-analysis has yet been published on the association between teenagers' use of pornography and gendered beliefs, but several studies have looked at associations between pornography use and the sexual objectification of women. Teenage pornography use has generally been associated with a strengthened belief that women are sex objects. Peter and Valkenburg (2009), for example, conducted a longitudinal study where teens were asked about their pornography consumption and agreement with statements such as "There is nothing wrong with boys being primarily interested in a woman's body." More frequent pornography use at first data collection was associated with a medium-sized increase in agreement with such statements a year later.

Tokunaga et al. (2019) meta-analyzed the findings of studies of the association between pornography use and participants' impersonal sexual attitudes (e.g., recreational attitudes toward sex) and behaviors (e.g., one night stands). Six of these studies included adolescent samples. The findings indicated a medium-sized association between pornography use and impersonal sexual attitudes and a slightly smaller but still significant association between pornography use and impersonal sexual behavior. In both cases, the use of pornography was associated with a more impersonal approach to sex.

The meta-analysis found that the findings of longitudinal studies were also positive, and four of the adolescent studies were longitudinal.

Finally, Wright et al. (2017) meta-analyzed the results of studies that explored correlations between teenagers' pornography use and body satisfaction (e.g., appearance ideals, physical self-esteem, genital satisfaction). Four of these studies sampled teenagers. Although certain individual studies did find that pornography use was associated with lower body satisfaction, the overall association when all the findings were aggregated together was not significant. The relationship between body satisfaction and pornography use, therefore, may be more nuanced and situation and person specific than for the previously described associations (e.g., between pornography use and impersonal sexual attitudes or notions of women as sex objects).

In conclusion, research on the nature of sexual scripts in pornography and their potential impact on teenagers has increased steadily in recent years. The question of causal inference can be approached with scientific rigidity or pragmatic realism. If a rigid and strictly scientific lens is adopted, the evidence of effects is highly suggestive, but not definitive. Through the lens of pragmatic realism, the evidence of effects is most certainly sufficient to deduce that pornography is a source of problematic sexual socialization for some youth and to conclude that potential solutions to prevent or counterbalance these negative impacts are warranted.

Potential Solutions
The most assured way to be unaffected by any type of problematic social influence is to avoid it or be oblivious to it. Some parents, for example, may attempt to use filtering software or device monitoring to prevent their teenagers from accessing pornography. Other parents may homeschool their children or stringently limit their access to peers or others who may show them pornography. This chapter adopts a position of neutrality on these and similar tactics. They are neither condemned nor condoned. However, it is the opinion of the author as well as many other health communication researchers that the most realistic approach to remediation involves increased pornography literacy. Given the data on teens' exposure to pornography, its ubiquity in cyberspace, and its ever increasing ease of access, education, rather than avoidance, is suggested as the most efficacious approach.

Media literacy training involves pedagogical activities designed to increase critical awareness about the production of particular media and the potential individual and social impacts of that media. Media literacy training programs have been developed for a number of topics, and meta-analysis indicates that as an educational genre they do have positive potential (Jeong et al., 2012). To the author's knowledge, however, only one media literacy training program has been developed and tested for pornography and teenagers, specifically: a nine-session curriculum called *The Truth about Pornography: A Pornography Literacy Curriculum for High School Students Designed to Reduce Sexual and Dating Violence* (Rothman et al., 2020).

This media literacy program was developed by public health scholars and educators in the United States with extensive knowledge about pornography as a medium, pornography as a source of social influence, and adolescent health. The curriculum was informed by scientific data and appropriate theoretical frameworks. Many aspects of the curriculum are directly relevant to the problematic sexual scripts discussed in this chapter. To illustrate, one component of the curriculum covers condom use, STIs, and pregnancy prevention. Another component covers body ideals. Other components cover topics such as gender roles and respectful behavior in dating and sexual relationships.

Albeit with only a small sample of adolescents, initial pre- and post-test data suggest the efficacy of this intervention. Significant shifts in attitudes were found in several key areas. Specifically, from pre- to post-test, adolescents were:

- Less likely to perceive pornography as a good way for young people to learn about sex
- More likely to perceive pornography as a potentially harmful social influence
- Less likely to believe women want to be called derogatory names during sex
- Less likely to believe people want to be physically aggressed against during sex
- Less likely to see pornography as realistic
- Less likely to want to emulate pornographic sex in their own lives

These findings are consistent with the results of a recent survey study of adolescents and young adults conducted in the Netherlands (Vandenbosch & van Oosten, 2017). This longitudinal panel analysis found that the association between more frequent pornography use and perceptions of women as sex objects was weaker when youth had received sex education in school that featured a component on pornography. Although the data were only correlational, they were consistent with the media literacy contention that educational efforts can attenuate negative media effects even when the media in question are still consumed. Also pertinent are the results of several studies of adults in various countries indicating that the association between pornography use and risk for having condomless sex is lessoned the more viewers perceive pornography as a less than optimal source of information about sex (e.g., Wright et al., 2018, 2019). In sum, although additional research is certainly needed, it appears that one potential avenue for remediating the harmful effects of pornography on teenagers in the area of sexual socialization is enhanced media literacy education.

Controversy II: Can Teenagers become "Addicted" to Pornography?

Research on Dysregulated Pornography Use

While the questions of pornography and sexual socialization in general and pornography's role in sexual violence perpetration in particular continue to be a source of controversy, many experts in the field would agree that they have been displaced by a newer controversy: the question of whether internet pornography (IP) can be "addicting." This debate is currently garnering far more research attention and rhetorical vehemence than any other question in the pornography effects domain. Grubbs et al. (2019) provide an excellent review of the history of this debate and its current status. The key points from their review are synopsized here.

First, although case reports of compulsive pornography use and its negative consequences appeared as early as the 1980s, it was not until the advent of IP that the public and the academic community began to discuss and research the notion of pornography addiction at scale. By this time, the idea that any type of sex could be "addicting" had already been debated by both practitioners and scholars, and some of these debates had included discussions of pornography. But several special affordances of IP—namely its accessibility, affordability, and anonymity—as well as concerns and reports of "internet addiction" (e.g., to gaming, shopping) more generally—led to a renewed and more expansive public debate and the commencement of a variety of scholarly papers and research studies. Theoretical models have since been proposed, labels have been debated, and data have been gathered using a host of scales. Field trial studies for the possible inclusion of a diagnosis of "hypersexuality" in the DSM-5 have found that problematic pornography use is the most common instantiation of out-of-control sexual behavior. In 2018, the newly released ICD-11 listed "Compulsive Sexual Behaviour Disorder" as a formal diagnosis.

In spite of these developments, controversy remains and dialogue (sometimes civil, sometimes not) about everything from etiology to terminology to diagnosis is ongoing. But there does seem to be a general consensus among the majority of researchers on the following points: some people's pornography use is dysregulated; some people report negative and severe consequences from their dysregulated pornography use; and some people identify themselves as pornography addicts.

Although research on teenagers is only just beginning, a recent dual-sample study by Kohut and Stulhofer (2018) suggests that teenagers are not immune from pornography related control problems. The teenage males in this longitudinal inquiry were tested for compulsive pornography use via agreement/disagreement with statements such as "I was upset because I could not stop thinking about pornography" and "I watched pornography even though I did not want to." Symptoms of compulsive pornography use such as these were associated with more intense usage rates in both samples. In one sample, 9% of males reported symptoms of highly dysregulated pornography use. In the other sample, 5% of males reported symptoms of highly dysregulated pornography use.

Thus, while debate about labeling continues (Is the appropriate moniker "addiction," "compulsion," "hypersexulaity," etc?), if the lived experience of study respondents and presenting clients is privileged over the skeptical eye of academics trepidatious about the reemergence of conservative "sex guilt" as a form of social control, it can be concluded that there is a small but still significant number of persons whose pornography use is dysregulated, that this dysregulation leads to a variety of personal and social problems, and that the affected population includes teenagers.

Potential Solutions

Sniewski et al. (2018) conducted a systematic review of the scholarly literature on the treatment of dysregulated pornography use. They were able to locate only 11 papers. Five of these were case studies of a single patient, and small sample sizes were the norm. Only one was a randomized control trial.

Not surprisingly, given the nascency of research in this area, Sniewski et al. (2018) were more likely to note limitations to the existing body of literature and suggest areas where future research is needed than to declare treatment recommendations for the problem of dysregulated pornography use. They did, however, note areas where solutions could potentially be found (albeit always cautioning that more research is needed).

First, they noted at a pharmacological level that the use of naltrexone may be efficacious. Three case studies had reported that their patient's pornography urges or use decreased following the introduction of naltrexone.

Second, they discussed how couples' therapy could be beneficial for persons in committed relationships struggling with dysregulated pornography use. These studies suggested that tactics designed to increase honesty, openness, trust, intimacy, and constructive conflict resolution within coupled relationships could, as a byproduct, lead to a reduced feeling of the need for pornography.

A third treatment modality recommended across several papers was therapeutic intervention for shame and guilt reduction. For some problematic pornography users, the guilt and shame they feel about their behavior initiates a cycle where the behavior both causes negative affect and relieves it, albeit temporarily, as it remerges due to the continuation of the behavior. By reducing shame and guilt, the urge to use pornography should decrease. Fourth, two studies were cited that used Acceptance and Commitment Therapy (ACT), including the one randomized control trial in the pool of papers. ACT emphasizes several cognitive and behavioral changes that appear to lead to enhanced pornography regulation, including accepting and observing pornography urges and negative affect rather than resisting or judging them, letting go of the need to control the self, situations, and others, identifying important values and goals and how pornography use inhibits them, and overtly committing to reducing pornography use.

Following Sniewski et al. (2018), this chapter emphasizes again that significant additions to the literature on the treatment of dysregulated pornography use are needed. This is especially true in the case of the present topic, as none of the treatment studies focused on teenagers. Nevertheless, the educational and public health communities should be open to the possibility that the findings to date on adults may generalize to younger persons. Medication can improve the mental health of teenagers as well as adults, for example, and few would dispute the general hypothesis that cognitive-behavior therapies for behavioral dysregulation can be effective for adolescents, not just adults.

Conclusion

The general question of whether pornography affects teenagers remains highly controversial, both within the scientific community and the lay public. The purpose of this chapter was to provide a straightforward, concise, and up-to-date review of the scholarly literature on the two most controversial questions: "Do teenagers learn problematic lessons about sex and self from pornography?" and "Can teenagers become 'addicted' to pornography?"

The pragmatic takeaways on these questions for educators are (a) there is sufficient evidence to conclude that some teenagers learn problematic lessons from pornography, (b) there is sufficient evidence to conclude that it is unlikely that teenagers are immune to the now well-documented problem of pornography dysregulation among adults, and (c) while additional research is needed, there are hopeful signs that remediating mechanisms to both these problems are available and increasing.

References

Bridges, A. J., Wosnitzer, R., Scharrer, E., Sun, C., & Liberman, R. (2010). Aggression and sexual behavior in best-selling pornography videos: A content analysis update. *Violence Against Women, 16*, 1065–1085. doi: 10.1177/1077801210382866

Fritz, N., & Paul, B. (2017). From orgasms to spanking: A content analysis of the agentic and objectifying sexual scripts in feminist, for women, and mainstream pornography. *Sex Roles, 77*, 639–652. doi: 10.1007/s11199-017-0759-6

Jeong, S. H., Cho, H., & Hwang, Y. (2012). Media literacy interventions: A meta-analytic review. *Journal of Communication, 62*, 454–472. doi: 10.1111/j.1460-2466.2012.01643.x

Kohut, T., & Stulhofer, A. (2018). The role of religiosity in adolescents' compulsive pornography use: A longitudinal assessment. *Journal of Sex & Marital Therapy, 44*, 759–775. doi: 10.1080/0092623X.2018.1466012

Peter, J., & Valkenburg, P. M. (2006). Adolescents' exposure to sexually explicit online material and recreational attitudes toward sex. *Journal of Communication, 56*, 639–660. doi: 10.1111/j.1460-2466.2006.00313.x

Peter, J., & Valkenburg, P. M. (2009). Adolescents' exposure to sexually explicit internet material and notions of women as sex objects: Assessing causality and underlying processes. *Journal of Communication, 59*, 407–433. doi: 10.1111/j.1460-2466.2009.01422.x

Rissel, C., Richters, J., De Visser, R. O., McKee, A., Yeung, A., & Caruana, T. (2017). A profile of pornography users in Australia: Findings from the second Australian study of health and relationships. *Journal of Sex Research, 54*, 227–240. doi: 10.1080/00224499.2016.1191597

Rothman, E. F., Daley, N., & Alder, J. (2020). A pornography literacy program for adolescents. *American Journal of Public Health, 110*, 154–156. doi: 10.2105/AJPH.2019.305468

Shor, E. (2019). Age, aggression, and pleasure in popular online pornographic videos. *Violence Against Women, 25*, 1018–1036. doi: 10.1177/1077801218804101

Sniewski, L., Farvid, P., & Carter, P. (2018). The assessment and treatment of problematic pornography use: A review. *Addictive Behaviors, 77*, 217–224. doi: 10.1016/j.addbeh.2017.10.010

Tokunaga, R. S., Wright, P. J., & Roskos, J. E. (2018). Pornography and impersonal sex. *Human Communication Research, 45*, 78–118. doi: 10.1093/hcr/hqy014

Tokunaga, R. S., Wright, P. W., & Vangeel, L. (2020). Is pornography a risk-factor for condomless sex? *Human Communication Research, 46,* 273–299. doi: 10.1093/hcr/hqaa005

Tylka, T. L. (2015). No harm in looking, right? Men's pornography consumption, body image, and well-being. *Psychology of Men & Masculinity, 16,* 97–107. doi: 10.1037/a0035774

Vandenbosch, L., & van Oosten, J. M. (2017). The relationship between online pornography and the sexual objectification of women: The attenuating role of porn literacy education. *Journal of Communication, 67,* 1015–1036. doi: 10.1111/jcom.12341

Vannier, S. A., Currie, A. B., & O'Sullivan, L. F. (2014). Schoolgirls and soccer moms: A content analysis of free "Teen" and "MILF" online pornography. *Journal of Sex Research, 51,* 253–264. doi: 10.1080/00224499.2013.829795

Wright, P. J., Sun, C., & Miezan, E. (2019). Individual differences in women's pornography use, perceptions of pornography, and unprotected sex: Preliminary results from South Korea. *Personality & Individual Difference, 141,* 107–110. doi: 10.1016/j.paid.2018.12.030

Wright, P. J., Sun, C., & Steffen, N. (2018). Pornography consumption, perceptions of pornography as sexual information, and condom use in Germany. *Journal of Sex & Marital Therapy, 44,* 800–805. doi: 10.1080/0092623X.2018.1462278

Wright, P. J., Tokunaga, R. S., & Kraus, A. (2016). A meta-analysis of pornography consumption and actual acts of sexual aggression in general population studies. *Journal of Communication, 66,* 183–205. doi: 10.1111/jcom.12201

Wright, P. J., Tokunaga, R. S., Kraus, A., & Klann, E. (2017). Pornography and satisfaction: A meta-analysis. *Human Communication Research, 43,* 315–343. doi: 10.1111/hcre.1210

CHAPTER 5

~

Lessons from the Dunedin Study

Helena M. McAnally and Robert J. Hancox

"I don't like television myself. I suppose its all right in small doses, but children never seem to be able to take it in small doses. They want to sit there all day long staring and staring at the screen..."

Willy Wonka in *Charlie & the Chocolate Factory*: Roald Dahl (1964)

Introduction

It is less than a century since television was invented and it wasn't until after the Second World War that television sets became widespread in people's homes. In this short time, spanning just three or four generations, television has profoundly changed human behavior. Leisure-time screen use has rapidly gone from zero hours per day to around 8 hours or more a day.

Estimates from the United States indicate that 13- to 18 year olds are typically exposed to between 8 and 10 hours of screen time per day, partly due to using multiple screens simultaneously (Rideout et al. 2010; Common Sense Media 2015). It is inconceivable that this profound change in human behavior has not had an impact on health and well-being.

Screen use may affect health and well-being in several ways. One is by displacing other activities: since there are limited hours in the day, time using screens reduces the time available to do other things. More screen time leaves less time for homework, exercise, play, or interacting with other people.

Screen time is also (usually) sedentary, and excessive sedentary behavior is bad for health. It is also likely that the content of screen time matters: for example, exposure to junk food advertising or unhealthy behaviors (such as violence or unsafe sex) are probably harmful for young people.

Concerns over the potential harms of excessive screen time on children's health and well-being are almost as old as television itself. Despite this, there has been surprisingly little research on the long-term effects of screen use. The Dunedin Multidisciplinary Health and Development Study (Dunedin Study) is unusual in that is has information on screen time during the childhood and adolescence of around 1000 children.

The Dunedin Study also has information on a broad range of physical and psychological health and well-being outcomes in adulthood, providing some of the best data anywhere in the world to assess the long-term impact of screen time.

Background

Dunedin Multidisciplinary Health and Development Study
Dunedin is home to New Zealand's oldest University (established in 1869). The city is in the lower South Island of New Zealand, with around 125, 000 residents, and is the main population center for the Otago region.

In the 1970s, Dunedin had one main maternity hospital, where most of the city's children were born. As part of a study into the influence of neonatal and perinatal circumstances on children's health and well-being, it was decided to follow-up a one-year cohort of children.

Of the 1661 live births between April 1972 and March 1973, 1,139 children were known to be residing in the Otago region and were eligible for inclusion in the follow up study at age three (McGee and Silva 1982; Poulton et al. 2015).One thousand and thirty seven children (91% of eligible births; 52% male) participated in this assessment forming the cohort for the study (McGee and Silva 1982). The cohort has been assessed at ages 5, 7, 9, 11, 13, 15, 18, 21, 26, 32, 38, and most recently at 45 years when 94.1% of the surviving 997 members were seen between 2017 and 2019.

The 1037 children reflected the demographic characteristics of Dunedin and represented the full range of socioeconomic status of New Zealand, although their families were was slightly wealthier on average and had fewer Māori (the tangata whenua or indigenous people of New Zealand) and other New Zealand cultures, as well as a smaller proportion of unwed mothers than was typical of New Zealand at this time (Buckfield 1978; McGee and Silva 1982; Reeder et al. 1994; Silva 1990).

Screen-Time Measures
At ages 5, 7, 9, and 11 years, parents were asked how much time Study members spent watching weekday television. At ages 13 and 15, Study members

themselves were asked how long they usually watched television on week-days and at weekends. The summary screen time measure used for most of the studies that are reported in this chapter was the average number of weekday viewing hours between ages 5 and 15 years.

The participants watched an average of 2.33 hours of television each weekday between the ages of 5 and 15 years. Girls watched slightly less than boys. From 1990 onwards, the American Academy of Pediatrics guidelines have consistently suggested limiting screen to no more than 1–2 hours of quality programming per day (American Academy of Pediatrics Committee on Public Education 2001; Strasburger et al. 2009, 2010; American Academy of Pediatrics 1990). However, the average TV viewing time in New Zealand exceeded this recommendation, even in the 1980s.

Despite this, the time that the Dunedin Study members spent watching television was far less than most surveys record for screen time in young people today (Common Sense Media 2015; Rideout et al. 2010; Twenge and Campbell 2018). The television and media environment has also changed in many other ways since the 1970s and 1980s when this cohort was growing up.

In contrast to today's rapidly evolving media environment, the Dunedin Study participants had a comparatively static and limited media environment when their TV viewing was measured (1977–1988) with television being the only significant screen-based option. There were only 2 state run televison channels in New Zealand at this time and neither ran for 24 hours a day. Few households had more than one television set.

Physical Health

Obesity
A frequent concern is that excessive screen use may lead to overweight and obesity by increasing sedentary behavior and stopping children from exercising. Children may also see a lot of advertisements for unhealthy food and drink, promoting an unhealthy diet. People also tend to eat more when they are distracted and overeating may be more likely when watching television during meal times.

Thus there are several ways in which screen use could influence body-weight, but does it? Many studies have found that people who watch more TV are more likely to be overweight or obese, but most studies can't tell us which comes first: it is possible that people who are already overweight chose to watch more TV.

The long follow-up of the Dunedin Study allows us to address this issue. The study found that more TV viewing in childhood was associated with a higher risk of being overweight or obese as assessed by body mass index (BMI) in adulthood even after taking childhood BMI into account (figure 5.1). It wasn't just that overweight children watched more TV: watching TV was associated with a long term risk of overweight and obesity in adulthood regardless of the children's BMI and more TV viewing was associated with more risk (Hancox et al. 2004).

This finding could not be explained by socioeconomic status or the BMI of the Dunedin Study members' parents either, suggesting that the association is a real effect and probably not due to other lifestyle factors. Remarkably, childhood TV viewing had a much stronger association with adult overweight/obesity than adult TV viewing. This suggests that the long-term effects of childhood TV on body weight are difficult to "undo" by reducing TV viewing in adulthood (Landhuis et al. 2008).

Fitness

Given that many of the same things that make excessive TV viewing a risk for obesity are also a risk for low levels of physical fitness, it also interesting to know whether childhood TV viewing and adult fitness were related. Perhaps

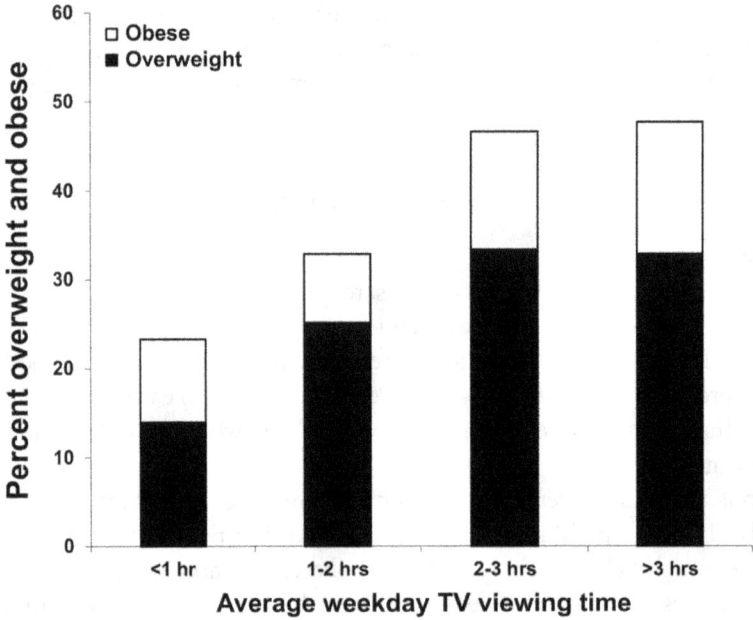

Figure 5.1 Prevalence of Overweight and Obesity at Age 26 according to Average Hours of Television Watching on Weekdays between Ages 5 and 15. Data from Hancox et al. (2004)

unsurprisingly, children who spent more time watching TV were more likely to be unfit as adults at age 26 or 32 years.

These findings could not be explained by differences in socioeconomic status (Hancox et al. 2004), although early childhood fitness could not be taken into account because this hadn't been measured. Like the findings for obesity, the Dunedin Study found that TV viewing in childhood was a stronger predictor of poor fitness in adulthood than adult TV viewing (Landhuis et al. 2008).

Smoking

Although direct advertising of cigarettes on TV was banned in the 1960s in New Zealand—before the Dunedin Study cohort was born—smoking imagery continued to feature prominently on television at the time that the participants were growing up, through product placement and tobacco sponsorship of sport.

In fact, TV viewing in childhood was associated with a greater risk of smoking by age 26 and that this association remained even after controlling for other factors that may be associated with taking up smoking including parental smoking and socioeconomic status (Hancox et al. 2004).

This finding may seem surprising given that as this cohort aged, they would have seen many public health advertisements about the harms of smoking than advertisements for cigarettes. It remains unclear why excessive TV viewing is linked to later smoking but further research with this cohort found that TV viewing is associated with several social and emotional issues. It may be smoking is a consequence of some of these other factors (see below).

Mental Health

Antisocial Behavior, Violence

The controversy over whether TV leads to antisocial behavior began before television broadcasts even started in New Zealand. The concern is that young people are likely to imitate the violence they observe on their screens, a concern that has increased with the onset of home video gaming, which is often very violent. Many studies show that children do become more aggressive or violent immediately after watching violent films, but whether this leads to long-term behavioral change is less clear.

On one side of the debate, some people argue that exposure to screen-based violence does not increase violence in real life. This argument seems reasonable given that a lot of violent content, such as cartoon violence, is very unlike reality. However human behavior is more complicated than simply copying observed behavior: children are good at drawing patterns of behavior or heuristics from their observations.

If violent responses to difficult situations are conveyed as appropriate and rewarded on screen, children may plausibly translate this into their own responses to their problems. This seems to be particularly likely when a hero perpetuates the violence. So when Batman uses violence to stop the Joker, it is seen as justifiable, whereas violence by the Joker towards Batman is not.

The Dunedin Study found that higher childhood and adolescent TV viewing time was associated with negative emotionality personality traits, as well as a greater likelihood of having diagnosis of antisocial personality disorder by age 26 (Robertson et al. 2013). Television viewing time was also associated with a higher likelihood of having a criminal conviction by age 26. For each extra hour of average weekday television, the risk of a criminal record increased by about 30% (see figure 5.2).

However, it was mostly non-violent crimes such as property damage, or theft that were related to childhood TV viewing (Robertson et al. 2013),

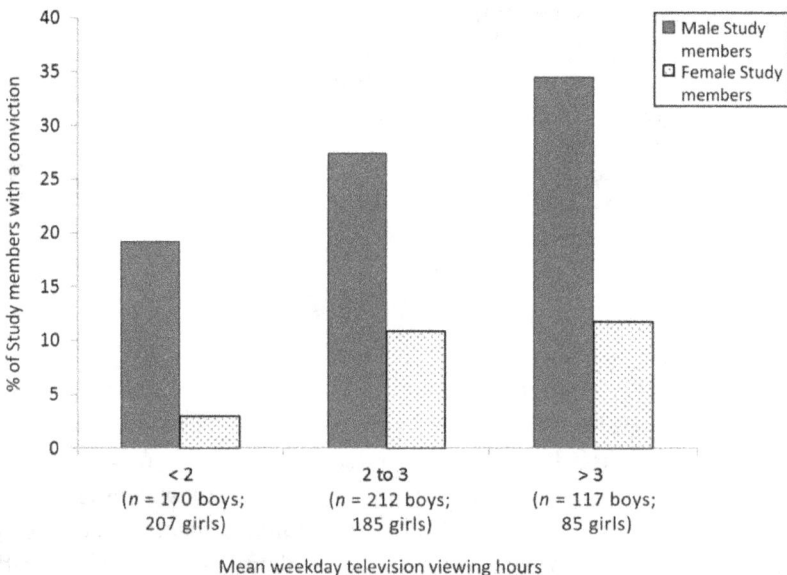

Figure 5.2 **Proportion of Male and Female Study Members with a Criminal Conviction by Age 26, by Mean Weekday Television Viewing between Ages 5 and 15 Years.** Reproduced with permission from Pediatrics 131, 439–466, Copyright © 2013 by the AAP

rather than violent crimes, which were much less common. This indicates that high levels of TV viewing are associated more generally with antisocial behavior, which is of concern. Furthermore, antisocial behavior increases the risk of criminal behavior and thus is a problem for society in terms of people's sense of safety and security. These findings suggest that reducing TV exposure in childhood may reduce the risk of committing crime in later life.

A limitation of this research is that what the Dunedin Study members were watching when they grew up is not known. Hence it is not clear whether those who watched the most television necessarily saw more violence or antisocial behavior. Nevertheless, violence and antisocial behaviors are so widely shown on television that it is certain that anyone spending substantial time watching television will have been exposed to these behaviors.

Internalizing Disorders
While there has been considerable debate about the effects of television viewing and externalizing behavior (such as antisocial behavior and violence), there has been much less interest in how television viewing might impact upon internalizing mental health disorders such as anxiety and depression. On the one hand excessive time watching television could plausibly lead to increased social anxiety and/or depression. On the other hand, it may be that people who are depressed or anxious chose to spend more time watching TV because this an activity that can be done at home allowing them to avoid social situations.

Again, the Dunedin Study can help to clarify this issue, because people do not usually develop internalizing disorders until their later teens or early twenties. Because the TV viewing times were gathered during childhood and adolescence, it seems unlikely that mental health disorders were causing children to watch more TV.

However, it remains possible that there are circumstances or personality traits that make it more likely that people will watch more TV *and* be more likely to develop problems with their mental health. Consequently, it is important to try and control for other factors that may be responsible for any observed associations when studying this issue.

The Dunedin Study has data on children's temperament from age five when both their parents and teachers reported on their worry and fearfulness. The research was also able to control for a selection of other factors that may have had an influence on the association between mental health outcomes and TV viewing. Analyses were adjusted for sex (women are more likely to have internalizing disorder as adults than men) and also socioeconomic status, as this is a predictor of later mental health outcomes.

The study found no relationship between childhood and adolescent TV viewing and later depression, as assessed when Study members were between 18 and 38. This finding remained regardless of whether TV viewing was assessed in childhood, adolescence or both. However, there was a relationship between TV viewing and anxiety (figure 5.3). Specifically, it seemed that higher rates of adolescent TV viewing were associated with later diagnosed anxiety (McAnally et al. 2019).

Although this association remained when early life worry or fearfulness was taken into account, the fact that the association was only found for adolescent television viewing leaves open the possibility that increased television viewing time might reflect increasing anxiety in adolescence rather than being a cause of anxiety.

Other research has suggested that excessive screen time is associated with depression (Twenge and Campbell 2018; Primack et al. 2009) and the lack of an association between television viewing and depression in the Dunedin Study may reflect the fact that the amount of television that the participants watched was far lower than young people's total leisure screen time today.

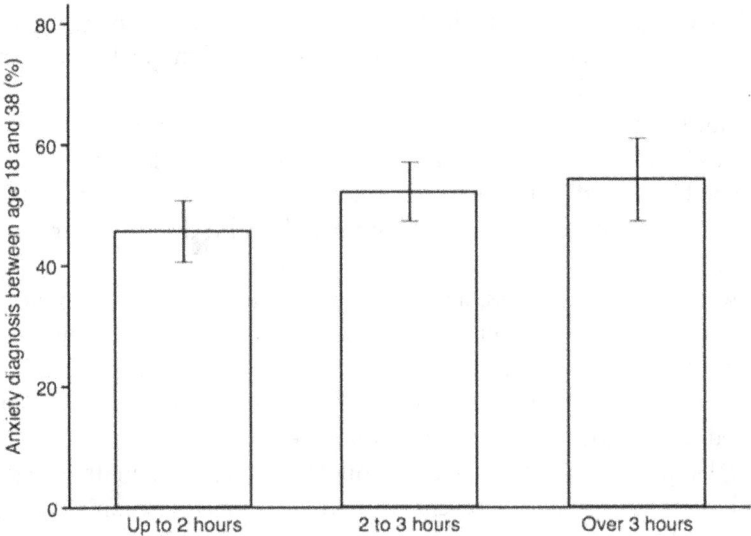

Figure 5.3 Diagnoses of Adult Anxiety Disorders according to Mean Childhood Television Viewing Time. Error Bars Show 95% Confidence Intervals: $p = 0.033$ for Trend across Groups. Reprinted from *Preventive Medicine Reports*, vol. 15. McAnally, Young, & Hancox. Childhood and adolescent television viewing and internalizing disorders in adulthood, article #100890. Copyright (2019), with permission from Elsevier.

Recent cross-sectional research, for example, has found associations between screen time and both anxiety and depression when screen time reached seven or more hours per day: the average screen time in this research was over four hours per day (Twenge and Campbell 2018), nearly double the amount of the Dunedin Study participants.

Attention

Too much television (or excessive screen time) is often blamed for children's perceived difficulties in paying attention. Is this actually the case? The Dunedin Study found that more screen time between ages 5 and 11 was associated with more attention problems in adolescence, as reported by both teachers and parents (Landhuis et al. 2007).

This finding persisted even after accounting for adolescent screen time at ages 13 and 15, suggesting that childhood TV viewing may have long-term impacts on attentional processes that have consequences for later achievement. It is important to note that these adolescent attention problems are not the same as Attention Deficit Hyperactivity Disorder (ADHD) diagnosis because, by definition, ADHD begins in early childhood.

Social Impacts

Education Achievement

Arguments about the educational effects of television viewing are also almost as old as television itself. Some argued that television was a powerful tool for teaching, while others suggested that it would distract from education. Given what is known about the link between screen time and attention problems, is there evidence that screen time has a detrimental effect on education outcomes? The Dunedin Study data indicate that there is.

Not only that, but watching television in childhood versus adolescence appeared to have slightly different effects on educational attainment. To summarize, more TV viewing between age 5 and 11 years was associated with a lower likelihood of obtaining a university degree by age 26, whereas, more adolescent TV viewing (age 13–15) was more strongly associated with leaving school without obtaining any educational qualifications (see figure 5.4: Hancox et al. 2005).

This association between television viewing and poor educational achievement could not be explained by either the families' socioeconomic status or children's cognitive abilities. In fact, when the impact of children's IQ was assessed, the strongest impact of television viewing on the chance

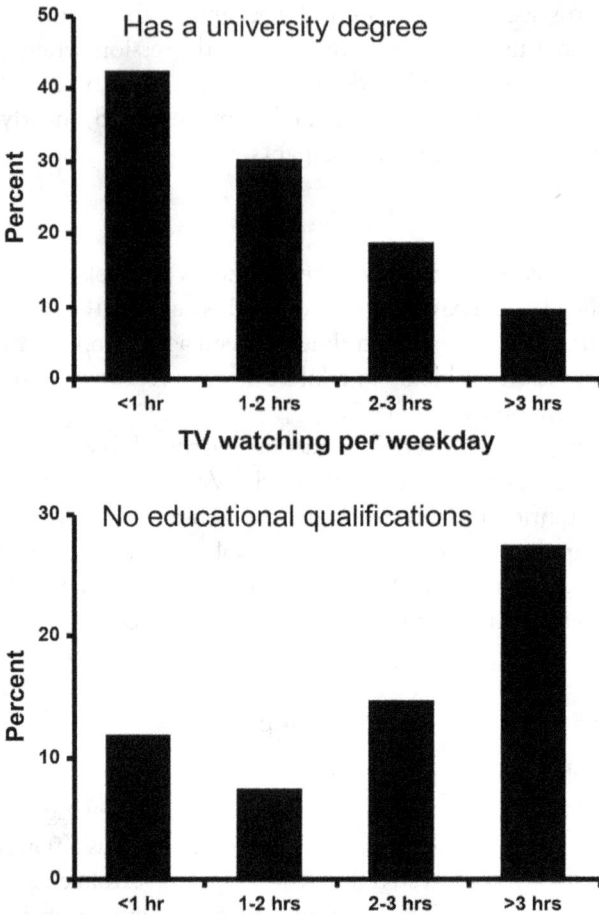

Figure 5.4   Child and Adolescent Television Viewing and Educational Achievement by 26 Years of Age. Television viewing is measured as unadjusted mean hours per weekday between 5 and 15 years of age. Data from Hancox et al. (2005).

of gaining a university degree was seen among those with average cognitive ability.

This makes sense—children with high IQs are likely to do well in education regardless of how much television they watch. The impact of television on higher education may be most obvious among those of average ability who are capable of doing well, but vulnerable to influences that impact on their education.

These findings indicate that while television may have educational potential in theory, the use of television in real life has few, if any, benefits on learning and educational success. In fact more time watching television appears to be detrimental. As well as the probable influence of too much television on attention skills, this may also be another effect of time displacement—time spent viewing TV leaves less time for studying, doing homework, reading for leisure, or any of a number of more educationally beneficial pursuits.

Unemployment

It was also hypothesized that the effects of TV viewing on educational attainment might mean that job security is harder to come by for those who have high childhood and adolescent TV viewing times. And this appears to be the case, although this was much stronger for the men in this cohort (figure 5.5).

Higher childhood or adolescent TV viewing among boys was associated with a higher risk of experiencing at least 6 months unemployment between ages 18 and 32. This association between unemployment and TV viewing was not entirely explained by poorer educational achievement: the higher risk of unemployment persisted even after taking educational achievement into account (Landhuis et al. 2012).

Interpersonal Relationships

An objection often raised against recommendations to reduce screen time, is that people will miss out on the shared experience of their age group. That is, young people will be disadvantaged by not being to talk about TV programs with their peers, which could make it difficult to make or maintain friendships. The same argument is sometimes made for improving family cohesiveness—watching TV together may help family members to bond.

Contrary to these arguments, the findings from the Dunedin Study show that those who watched less television actually had stronger relationships with both parents and peers than those with higher screen time (Richards et al. 2010). This is despite the fact that the Dunedin TV data were collected at a time when most families had only one TV set, so TV was more likely to be a family activity. The detrimental effects of excessive screen time on interpersonal relationships may be worse today because most households have multiple screens and many different forms of media, meaning that families and friends are unlikely to be watching the same programs.

Although the social nature of screen use has changed considerably since the Dunedin Study participants were growing up, it seems unlikely that the value of real life (as distinct from on-screen) social interaction has. It is possible that reducing screen time overall is more likely to improve interpersonal relationships than cause difficulties.

a

Hours of weekday TV viewing by girls between ages 5 to 15 years

b

Hours of weekday TV viewing by boys between ages 5 to 15 years

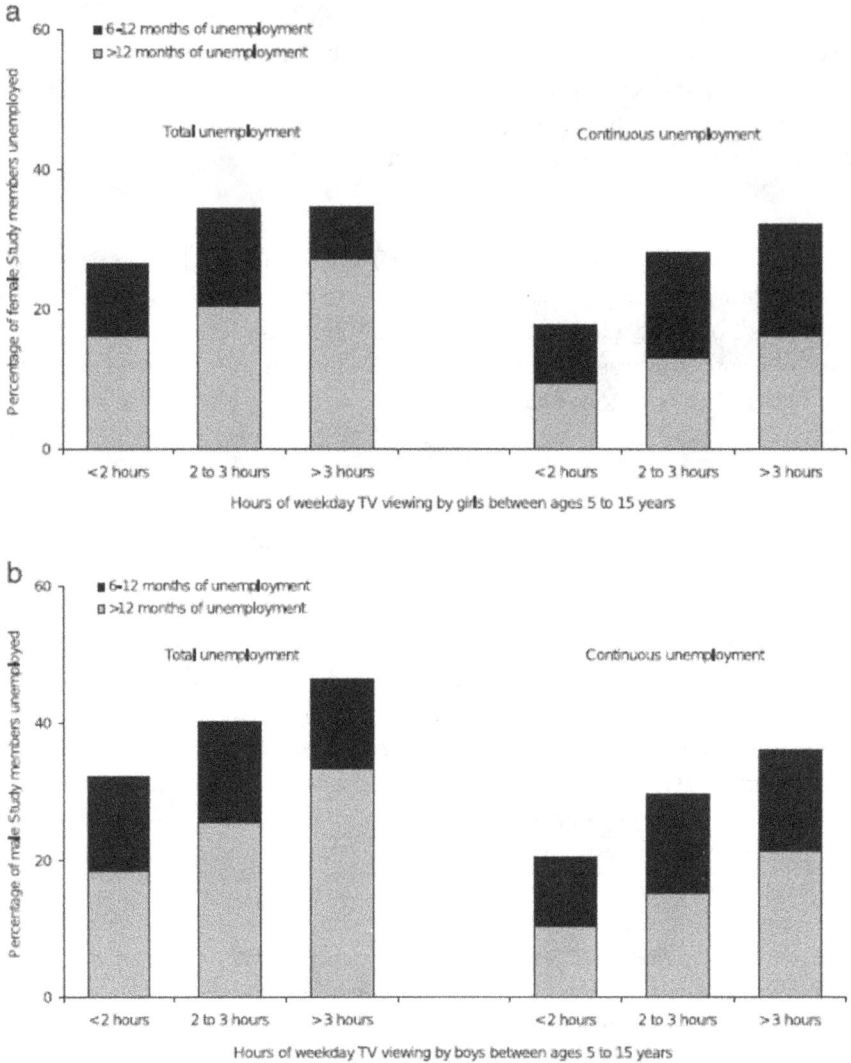

Figure 5.5 Proportion of Study members That Reported At Least 6 Months, or At Least 12 Months of Unemployment between Ages 18 and 32 Years, as a Function of Childhood and Adolescent Weekday Television Viewing. Results include total months of unemployment (the cumulative month of unemployment between 18 to 32 years) and longest period of continuous unemployment (the longest unbroken period of unemployment). Results presented separately for female (a) and male (b). Study members in New Zealand between 1972 and 2005. Reprinted from Preventive Medicine, 54(2), Landhuis, Perry & Hancox, Association between childhood and adolescent television viewing and unemployment in adulthood, 168–173., Copyright (2012), with permission from Elsevier.

Conclusions

The Dunedin Study shows us that excessive screen use (in the form of TV viewing) during childhood and adolescence is associated with several undesirable outcomes both during adolescence and extending into in adulthood. These outcomes occur across the whole spectrum of human health and well-being, from physical health to mental health to education, work, and interpersonal relationships. With the exception of adult depression, for which no association was found, all of the associations that were observed were harmful: higher TV viewing was always associated with poorer outcomes.

Typically these associations were observed in those who watched more than two hours of television per day. As these poorer outcomes were predicted by the average number of hours of TV viewed, these findings suggest that reducing screen use would have lasting benefits for young people. Since 1990, the American Academy of Pediatrics has recommended limiting screen time to less than two hours per day (American Academy of Pediatrics Committee on Public Education 2001; Strasburger et al. 2009, 2010; American Academy of Pediatrics 1990) and the findings of the Dunedin Study suggest that this is a good target to aim for.

Not all of these adverse effects of television were necessarily expected. There are several plausible ways in which TV viewing could have been beneficial. Without question, TV is an excellent communicator of information and access to informative programs such as documentaries could spark curiosity and lead to better education outcomes.

Shared enjoyment of TV shows could have strengthened friendships and family ties, and exposure to different characters and world views could have increased empathy. All of these potentially positive outcomes have been suggested by advocates for the benefits of television, but none of these benefits were observed in the Dunedin Study members.

Are the Findings Believable?

Some critics have argued that the negative associations observed in this research could be caused by other influences—and due to bad parenting in particular. In other words, relationships between negative outcomes and TV occurred simply because "bad parents" let their children watch more television. However, this begs the question of why "good" parents limit TV use. Presumably they do so because they believe that TV viewing times should be limited.

The comprehensive nature of data in the Dunedin Study also meant that factors such as socioeconomic status and aspects of parenting style that might provide other explanations for the findings could be controlled for. Even after taking these factors into account, the observed negative effects held.

Furthermore, these findings are in keeping with other research that shows the short term, negative effects of TV viewing (see Strasburger et al. 2009, 2010 for an overview of some of these shorter term associations). The long-term follow-up of the Dunedin Study shows that these short-term effects persist and that the consequences of excessive childhood and adolescent TV viewing may be long lasting.

Limitations

Although television only arrived in Dunedin 10 years before the Study cohort was born, TV rapidly became so ubiquitous that all of the participants watched TV. Despite this, the average viewing time was far lower than the screen viewing times observed in more recent research (see for example, Twenge and Campbell 2018). Not only has the amount of screen use increased, but there is much wider variety of screen content and screen use behavior now than there was in the past.

Although the Dunedin Study shows that excessive screen time is associated with long-lasting negative consequences, it doesn't show the extent to which these effects depend on the content of screen use (quality). Researchers cannot investigate whether different types of screen use would have different effects, since the cohort grew up in a world with very little (if any) access to other forms of personal-screen entertainment. Lastly, there is no information on screen use among very young children. This is a concern because children under five years of age are increasingly exposed to a wide variety media (see Radesky and Christakis 2016).

Screen use behavior has also changed dramatically since the Dunedin data were collected. Despite this, the majority of young people still report at least some daily television watching (Common Sense Media 2015), as well as using newer forms of screen-based media.

It remains to be seen how new media will impact on long-term health and well-being but cross-sectional evidence is already suggests that the short-term effects are similar to those observed in the Dunedin Study data (e.g., Guerrero and Forment 2019). The quantity of young people's screen use has increased substantially since the Dunedin study's generation and it seems likely that these findings under-estimate the potential harm caused by excessive screen use in today's screen use environment.

Solutions

Although the screen-based media environment we have today may have many benefits when used moderately, the evidence suggests *excessive* screen use has multiple long-term harms. This is unsurprising: many behaviors are harmless or beneficial in moderation but become harmful in excess. The Dunedin data show that screen use should be moderated and that reasonable use (less than two hours per day for leisure time use) is unlikely to be harmful.

The question then is how can we moderate or reduce children's screen use? Adults can take a lead in this by modeling moderate screen use. Many adults now spend most of their working day on a computer and then watch television or use social media at home, perhaps spending three quarters of their waking hours in front of a screen.

Parents and teachers can also advocate to their schools and school boards about policies in relation to screen time. This could take the form of device-free school yards (i.e., no personal devices during free time at school) or requiring a school to commit to a percentage of device free classroom time (there is no good evidence that young people learn better from screens than from more traditional teaching methods).

Teaching media literacy is also crucially important. In a time where social-media platforms are global and extremely lucrative it is necessary for students to think critically about their screen and media use and who is benefiting from it. There is now compelling evidence that excessive screen use has widespread personal costs to health and well-being, yet we are currently in an environment where strategies to encourage high screen use are being used by a number of media use organizations (see Guerrero and Forment 2019).

Lastly, given the health effects associated with screen time, it seems important that governments and public health agencies make sure that we, as a society, benefit from the media environment. This may include regulating large companies that make money from people's screen engagement.

Public health agencies have put great effort into advocating for smoking cessation, healthier eating, and safe sexual practices: similar campaigns could be used to advocate for safe screen use. While there are many benefits to the current screen use environment, it is important to remember that when it comes to health and well-being, all things (including screen time) in moderation is a good rule of thumb.

Acknowledgments

We would like to thank the participants of the Dunedin Study and their families and friends for their on-going support of this research and their generosity in sharing a lifetime of information with us. We would also like to thank the research teams who collected the data, the Principal Investigators who shared their data, the Dunedin Study founder Dr Phil Silva, and the current director Professor Richie Poulton. The Dunedin Study is supported by the Health Research Council of New Zealand.

References

American Academy of Pediatrics. 1990. "Children, adolescents, and television." *Pediatrics* 85(6): 1119–1120.

American Academy of Pediatrics Committee on Public Education. 2001. "Children, adolescents, and television." *Pediatrics* 107(2): 423–426.

Buckfield, P. M. 1978. "Perinatal events in the Dunedin city population 1967–1973." *New Zealand Medical Journal* 88: 244–246.

Common Sense Media. 2015. "Landmark report: U.S. teens use an average of nine hours of media per day, tweens use six hours." https://www.commonsensemedia.org/aboutus/news/press-releases/landmark-report-us-teens-use-an-average-of-nine-hours-ofmedia-per-day.

Dahl, R. 1964. *Charlie and the Chocoloate Factory.* New York: Alfred A. Knopf, Inc.

Guerrero, M. J. C., and M. A. Forment. 2019. "Coping with and addressing the risks of children TV and online devices usage." Seventh International Conference on Technological Ecosystems for Enhancing Multiculturality (TEEM 2019), León, Spain.

Hancox, R. J., B. J. Milne, and R. Poulton. 2004. "Association between child and adolescent television viewing and adult health: A longitudinal birth cohort study." *Lancet* 364(9430): 257–262.

Hancox, R. J., B. J. Milne, and R. Poulton. 2005. "Association of television viewing during childhood with poor educational achievement." *Archives of Pediatrics & Adolescent Medicine* 159(7): 614–618.

Landhuis, C. Erik, David K. Perry, and Robert J. Hancox. 2012. "Association between childhood and adolescent television viewing and unemployment in adulthood." *Preventive Medicine* 54(2): 168–173. doi: 10.1016/j.ypmed.2011.11.007.

Landhuis, C. Erik, Richie Poulton, David Welch, and Robert J. Hancox. 2007. "Does childhood television viewing lead to attention problems in adolescence? Results from a prospective longitudinal study." *Pediatrics* 120(3): 532–537. doi: 10.1542/peds.2007-0978.

Landhuis, C. Erik, Richie Poulton, David Welch, and Robert J. Hancox. 2008. "Programming obesity and poor fitness: The long-term impact of childhood television." *Obesity* 16(6): 1457–1459. doi: 10.1038/oby.2008.205.

McAnally, H. M., T. Young, and R. J. Hancox. 2019. "Childhood and adolescent television viewing and internalising disorders in adulthood." *Preventive Medicine Reports* 15: 100890. doi: 10.1016/j.pmedr.2019.100890.

McGee, R., and P. A. Silva. 1982. "A thousand New Zealand children: Their health and development from birth to seven." In *Special Report Series No. 8*. Dunedin: Medical Research Council of New Zealand.

Poulton, Richie, Terrie E. Moffitt, and Phil A. Silva. 2015. "The Dunedin Multidisciplinary Health and Development Study: Overview of the first 40 years, with an eye to the future." *Social Psychiatry and Psychiatric Epidemiology* 50(5): 679–693. doi: 10.1007/s00127-015-1048-8.

Primack, Brian A., Brandi Swanier, Anna M. Georgiopoulos, Stephanie R. Land, and Michael J. Fine. 2009. "Association between media use in adolescence and depression in young adulthood: A longitudinal study." *Archives of General Psychiatry* 66(2): 181–188. doi: 10.1001/archgenpsychiatry.2008.532.

Radesky, J., and D. Christakis. 2016. "Media and young minds: Policy statement of the American Academy of Pediatrics." *Pediatrics* 138(5): e20162591.

Reeder, A. I., M. Feehan, D. J. Chalmers, and P. A. Silva. 1994. "Some socio-economic characteristics of a much-studied cohort: The Dunedin Multidisciplinary Health and Development Study." *New Zealand Journal of Education Studies* 29: 209–213.

Richards, Rosalina, Rob McGee, Sheila M. Williams, David Welch, and Robert J. Hancox. 2010. "Adolescent screen time and attachment to parents and peersscreen time and attachment to parents and peers." *JAMA Pediatrics* 164(3): 258–262. doi: 10.1001/archpediatrics.2009.280.

Rideout, V., U. Foehr, and D. Roberts. 2010. *Generation M2: Media in the Lives of 8 to 18-Year-Olds*. Menlo Park, CA: Kaiser Family Foundation.

Robertson, L. A., H. M. McAnally, and R. J. Hancox. 2013. "Childhood and adolescent television viewing and antisocial behavior in early adulthood." *Pediatrics*. doi: 10.1542/peds.2012-1582.

Silva, P. A. 1990. "The Dunedin Multidisciplinary Health and Development Study: A 15 year longitudinal study." *Paediatric and Perinatal Epidemiology* 4: 76–107.

Strasburger, V. C., Amy B. Jordan, and Ed Donnerstein. 2010. "Health effects of media on children and adolescents." *Pediatrics* 125(4): 756. doi: 10.1542/peds.2009-2563.

Strasburger, V. C., B. J. Wilson, and A. B. Jordan. 2009. *Children, Adolescents and the Media*. 2nd ed. Thousand Oaks, CA: SAGE.

Twenge, Jean M., and W. Keith Campbell. 2018. "Associations between screen time and lower psychological well-being among children and adolescents: Evidence from a population-based study." *Preventive Medicine Reports* 12: 271–283. doi: 10.1016/j.pmedr.2018.10.003.

CHAPTER 6

~

The Rise and Fall of Screen Time

Sonia Livingstone

"Parents: Don't Let the Screens Win" (*Wall Street Journal*, 4/28/20)

"Too Much Screen Time? Here's How to Dial Back" (*New York Times*, 12/14/19)

"There's Worrying New Research about Kids' Screen Time and Their Mental Health" (*Time*, 10/29/18)

"Screen Time May Actually Be Good for Kids" (*Forbes*, 10/22/19)

"We've Got the Screen Time Debate All Wrong. Let's Fix It" (*Wired*, 12/20/18)

In the battle between parents and screen media, parents will struggle. When screen time becomes a battle between parents and children, everyone loses. Parents are constantly told that too much screen time turns children into zombies, makes them obese, destroys their chance of academic success, and more. The solution, they are also told, is to impose "screen time rules." Yet these rules are controversial among scientists for relying on contested evidence. They are also controversial as policy advice, for their purpose is unclear and the results of implementing them untested. They are certainly controversial in family life.

In one sense, the screen time controversy is centuries-old, for deep anxieties about technological and social change go back to Plato's worry that writing would erase memory, to the Catholic church's fear that the printing press would undermining its authority by democratizing access to knowledge, and to public anxieties over the circus, comic books, the cinema, radio—each in turn feared for unleashing the unruly or immoral impulses of the weak-willed. Traditionally, these were women, children, and the working classes, though at the turn of the twentieth century, "children were being redefined sympathetically as innocent and impressionable, a departure from earlier Calvinist conceptions of children as evil barbarians in need of discipline" (Butsch, 2000: 152).

In another sense, the screen time controversy is modern—reliant on the emergence of the discipline of psychology and its embrace of statistical techniques pioneered in relation to mass media by market research organizations to price and sell screen time to advertisers (by measuring audience attention or "eyeballs"). The result was innovative ways to measure and track trends in the population's behavior, even in the privacy of their homes, and to correlate these with body weight or school grades or crime rates or any other societal problem of the day. While this enabled the development of public policy concerned with child welfare, it obscured the significance of screen content, meanings or contexts of use in the everyday lives of children.

This chapter argues that, instead of trying to resolve the screen time controversy, it is time to leave it behind as ill-founded. Although claims for and against screen time continue to make the headlines, for even old controversies sell stories, I suggest that the concept of screen time has led scientists, policy makers and the public down a blind alley, wasting a vast amount of energy that could have been better directed toward supporting children's well-being in a mediated world.

Screen Time Controversies in the Family

One mother, during an interview for our book, *Parenting for a Digital Future* (Livingstone & Blum-Ross, 2020), interrupted us to call to her 14-year old son doing his homework in the next room—"Have you turned your *Self-Control* on?" It turned out that the laptop his school had given him to take home was preloaded with a screen time app. Meanwhile mother had her own app called *K9* (after the police sniffer dogs) to manage her children's digital activities. We came away from that family concerned that, when we asked the mother about parenting style, she unhappily called herself a "police-woman."

In other families, a father of a 15-year old son with autism told us that he was trying to "cut [screen time] down... until it's at a manageable level, which should be no more than two hours." The mother of an 8- and 10-year old told us "in the news I heard...no more than two hours." Another mother complained, we've got so much information now, about screen time is bad, or just stuff pumped at us; you sort of feel guilty if you let them have ...yes, if you let them have too much." Another was "pulling her hair out" trying to find the right "level of exposure" for her 12-year old video-gaming son.

The mother of a wakeful three-year old and a new baby told us how she started each day feeling guilty about breaking the screen time rules when she handed her three-year old child the tablet first thing in the morning so as to get the household up and ready for the day. And yet another told us that "the conversation about screen time is a big thing, because I think a lot of parents worry firstly about how long is OK and secondly about the impact".

This research was conducted in London with families from many walks of life, and we were struck by how often we heard some version of the American Academy of Pediatrics' (AAP) "2x2" screen time rules (no screen time for children under two years old; no more than two hours for older children). These usually surfaced unattributed in our interviews, applied to all kinds of screen media, although they were originally intended for American parents trying to manage their children's television viewing. Notably, they were more often cited as a source of difficulty and guilt than of solace. Zaman et al. (2020) similarly document how public discourse in Australia also refers to parents feeling blamed, guilty, judged, worried about their digital parenting.

In short, irrespective of the original intent behind the screen time rules, in practice these rules have become a problem. While the rules promise an authorized way to cut short seemingly unending family disputes, the result is often the opposite. Allowing or withdrawing digital technologies has become parents' go-to reward or punishment; consequently, it has also become children's chosen battlefield to assert their agency. Our national survey of British parents found that they were far more concerned about screen *time* than about the actual activities their children engaged in online (or many of their offline activities; Livingstone & Blum-Ross, 2020). Parent-child conflict generates evasion by children, as illustrated by our discovery that the children in the first family mentioned above had figured out how to get the tablets out of the household safe in the middle of the night.

Also problematic are the implications for family relations. If "good parenting" is "policing" screen time, what are children—criminals? Parenting guidance and media headlines are full of injunctions to police: control, ban, monitor, and spy on children. This undermines family harmony, and the efforts of recent generations to rethink family dynamics —to become less hierarchical, less gendered, and more democratic. After all, children are neither ignorant nor wicked but, rather, keen to participate in family decision making, positive when their agency is respected, frustrated when it is not.

Recently the screen time rules have been "app-ified," as illustrated by the first mother above. This not only points to a problem experienced by parents but also to the very considerable market in promised solutions (parental controls), a market that, as critics put it, first created and now profits from parental paranoia (Lee et al., 2014). Now that the iPhone comes with a Screen Time app pre-installed, our lives and those of our children are constantly quantified, monitored and, indeed, commodified by those who trade in the data collected.

Yet none of this resolves the pressing ambivalence that many parents feel, since as well as restricting screen time, they feel urgently that they must equip their child for the digital world. It is this, as much as their children's demands, that leads them to acquire all the digital devices they can afford, to help their child "keep up," "get ahead," prepare for the jobs not yet invented that supposedly await them in the digital future. As one middle-class mother told us, on the one hand she was so anxious about the "tsunami" of devices in the home that she kept a spreadsheet to control her 12-year old daughter's Internet use, but on the other she wanted to support her daughter learning Scratch at school, sharing poems online, and more broadly having the chance to experiment and gain resilience online and offline. Other parents worried about homework or shopping online, video chat with grandparents, or staying in touch with distant family. "What counts" as screen time, they asked us? Where's the flexibility?

So how did this sorry situation come about? While one could go back further in terms of research on children and screens, to the days of cinema, attention to whether screen time displaces valuable childhood activities really began with the arrival of television.

Early Research on Children and Television

No informed person can say simply that television is bad or that it is good for children.

This is the first sentence of Schramm, Lyle, and Parker's seminal book, *Television in the Lives of Our Children*, published in 1961 just as television was becoming a mass phenomenon for American families, and as the public and policy makers were becoming anxious about yet another technological revolution. In setting out their research, they observed that "the most serious and frequent question raised about television is this": *Does its violence teach children violence and crime?* Their conclusions were noteworthy (though not great material for the headlines) and, by and large, they have stood the test of time: "the relationship is always between a *kind* of television and a *kind* of child in a *kind* of situation" (p.169).

Schramm et al. asked, further, does television make children aggressive? Answer: It depends on their circumstances: "Children who come to television with aggression will be more likely to remember aggressive acts and be able to apply them when they are aggressive in real life" (p.163). Does it make them mentally ill? Again, it depends on the child: "We see no evidence whatsoever that television *makes* a child withdrawn, or *makes* passivity. Rather, it encourages and reinforces those tendencies *when they exist in dangerous amounts*" (p.160).[1]

Pipping Schramm et al. to the post was another influential book. *Television and the Child* was published in the UK by Himmelweit, Oppenheim, and Vince in 1958. It set the mold for innumerable studies responding to society's worries about media representations of violence and its potential to make children aggressive, along with anxieties about "addiction" and adverse effects on children's reading, health, and school work. Its conclusions were similarly qualified, however, pointing more to the factors in a child's life that influence their response to television than to television's "impact" on them. Certainly, Himmelweit et al. did not conclude that television made children "passive"—somewhat testily, they distinguished at least five possible meanings of this popular claim before pointing to the evidence to rebut each in turn. But perhaps they raised questions in the public mind by distinguishing displacement effects (the activities that are reduced to make time for viewing) from the effects of program content. And Schramm et al. raised similar questions that struck a chord with the American public.

As it turned out, the UK findings for displacement effects were equivocal, with a range of contextual factors making it difficult to conclude that, say, television reduced book reading or seeing friends. While their findings were more marked, albeit with differences measured in minutes not hours per day, Schramm et al. concluded dramatically that:

> Comparing pretelevision with television communities, we saw that the new medium reorganizes leisure time and mass media use in a spectacular manner. It cuts deeply into movie-going, radio-listening, comic book and pulp magazine reading. It reduces the time for play. It postpones bedtime slightly. It dominates the child's leisure. (p. 69)

With the benefit of hindsight, we can see that, although children still read, sleep, play, and see their friends—and, crucially, not notably less than they did half a century ago—television's reorganization of our daily lives and, as parents often observe, of their children's attention and interests, has indeed been spectacular. No wonder time spent on viewing, and the time consequently less available for other activities, raise concerns. Now that the Internet has yet further reorganized our lives, encompassing not only our leisure time but also time spent on education, work, commerce, and civic participation, these concerns are far from laid to rest.

Time as the Problem

Neither of these agenda-setting books used the term "screen time" (though Schramm et al. did mention "mass communication time" when summing the time children spent on television and radio). But they did address concerns about screen time as well as about screen content, and thus they can be judged part of the cultural problematization of time that is inherent in the idea of screen time.

A quarter of a century on, and now approaching the end of the heyday of television, the research agenda was little changed. For sure, a wealth of studies had expanded the array of contextual factors understood to affect the relation between viewing and effects, and "the child" had gained more of a voice and a personality in the family. For example, Dorr's (1986) "Television and Children" found that "viewing time" displaced just a few daily minutes of sleep, homework, and unstructured outdoor play, though it did not displace adult-directed activities such as school, chores, or extracurricular activities. Acknowledging the many qualifications attached to the claim that either viewing time or television content harms children, Dorr concluded instead with a concern that time spent viewing offers little improvement in children's lives since most of what they watch "was not designed with children's welfare in mind, and some of it is decidedly aggressive, sexist, ageist, racist, consumption oriented, sexy, inane, or moronic" (p.82).

Note how the two hypotheses—that viewing time displaces other (better) activities, and that viewing problematic content has adverse effects on children's attitudes or behavior - easily become entangled. For measuring viewing time is much simpler than keeping track of exactly what children watch, let alone how they interpret it. In other words, for researchers seeking reliable measures, viewing time offers a simple proxy for media content, since viewing particular (violent, stereotyped) content takes up time. After all, it seems reasonable to assume that the more time spent viewing, the greater the effects of the content.

Yet although a voluminous body of research has explored this hypothesis, generally reporting a modest correlation, few studies eliminate confounding factors or control for third causes. When the latter are included in study designs, it generally turns out that influential factors in the child's background (socio-economic status, family difficulties, emotional problems) are linked both to greater viewing and to the child's (aggressive, stereotyped) attitudes or behavior. As Schramm et al. observed decades earlier.

But measuring children's attitudes and behaviors is difficult, especially using carefully controlled research designs. So viewing time came to offer a proxy not only for media content but also for media effects. Hence the headlines—"Two hours gaming!" "Boys spend more hours viewing than girls!" "Children view for longer than ever before!" As if measuring time spent is in and of itself evidence of a problem.

But what problem? Consider the many studies reporting a link between time spent viewing television and childhood obesity, sparked by the evident increase in both during the post-war decades. As the experts concede, not only is the observed correlation inconsistent and small, but it remains unexplained, for neither the cause nor the effect are clearly specified (Cairns et al., 2019).

Is the problem that more time spent viewing displaces physical activity, or that it exposes the child to more junk food advertisements and, thus, different attitudes to food, or that while they are viewing they tend to snack more? Research has not disentangled these, nor has it adequately addressed the alternative explanations, notably the hypothesis that poorer children can't access parks and play streets so stay home and watch more television and, also, poorer children live in food deserts with parents working shifts, so their diet includes more junk food. Yet these matter when deciding to build more sporting facilities, or pass stronger advertising regulation, or impose a sugar tax or, most radical, provide more resources for poorer families.

The Invention of "Screen Time"

Writing in 2008 about moral panics accompanying the introduction of each new medium, Critcher observes that arguments about television's displacement of other activities are "dwarfed in importance by the one dominant accusation, that violence on television begets violence in real life." (p.97). Yet the discourse was already changing. Figure 6.1 shows the results of a Google Trends analysis, based on all US online searches, for the maximum time period that the analysis allows. First, I searched for mention of "screen time." After some experimentation, it seemed that Critcher was right; what really gathered interest in relation to children and media before screen time was "media violence" (as Schramm et al. had observed some decades earlier).

The timeline in figure 6.1 is telling. At least since 2004, and possibly earlier, interest in media violence has been steadily falling, though it seems unlikely that either violent content or, indeed, the problem of violence in

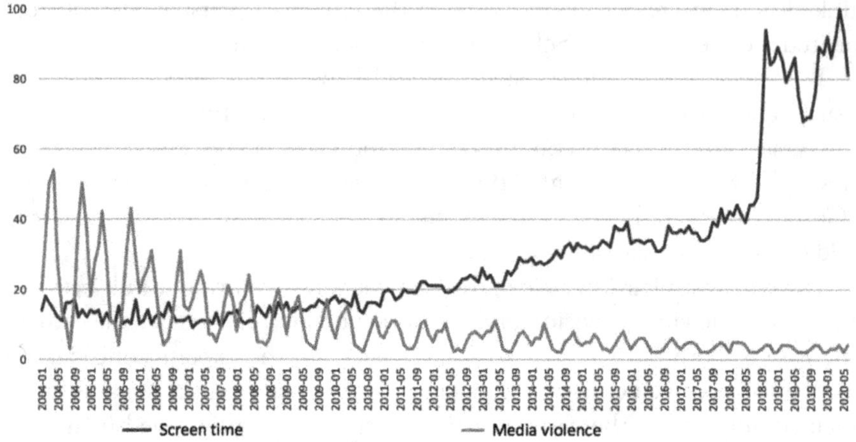

Figure 6.1　Screen Time Takes Over from Media Violence. Google Trends analysis

society, has been falling over this period. Meanwhile, through the same period, interest in screen time has been rising, at first steadily, but faster over the past decade than the one before, and with a striking jump in 2018.

What's going on? Explaining that "contemporary calls to reduce screen time are rooted in the 'television-free' movement that first emerged in the 1970s," Alper observes that as early as May 1975, when "reporting on the 1971 National Symposium on Children and Television, sponsored by the parent group Action for Children's Television, the *Hartford Courant* led with the headline 'Screen Time Calculated'" (2014: 20, 21). Notwithstanding this early mention, a search of the online news database Nexis reveals that for most of television's history, building on the influence of the cinema, the term "screen time" meant time on the screen—as in discussions of how special effects dominated a film's screen time, or how a fight took seven minutes of screen time, or actors battling for screen time, or the amount of screen time occupied by advertising.[2]

Everyday terminology only began to shift in the 1990s. In the May–June 1991 edition of Mother Jones Magazine, Tom Engelhardt wrote an article wittily entitled "The Primal Screen" in which, echoing Schramm et al., he expressed concern that "the screen offers only itself as an organizing principle for children's experience" (p.69), such that screen time has become more real for children than "real time." Though Engelhardt's concern was more with the quality than the quantity of viewing time, he distinguished what is on-screen from screen time, using the latter to refer to the daily hours that children sit in front of the multiple screens in the modern American home.[3]

Authoritative Rules Limiting Screen Time

From the early 1990s onwards, screen time, initially put in quotation marks, was increasingly used to refer to the time a person (in fact from the start, a child) spends in front of the screen, while the former usage was increasingly marked out as "on-screen time." After all, that was the decade in which television itself was being taken over by digital media of several kinds, each jostling for attention with television, often by being literally plugged into it (think of the video recorder or games console or early home computer).

A new terminology was needed—"viewing" no longer captured all the ways that children engaged with screens; "television" was no longer the only medium; people's time (and attention) was being commodified by a multi-media marketplace; and parents were more anxious about what was widely called "new media" than about the suddenly-familiar television. Researchers too were seeking new ways to measure all these different forms of media use, and several academic reports on the amount of time children spent on all the media available in the home gained significant press attention.[4]

In 1999 the Committee on Public Education of the AAP published an influential report on Media Education. It noted evidence linking children's time spent on television and other media to (1) the displacement of creative, active, or social pursuits; (2) aggressive and sexualized behavior, (3) tobacco and alcohol consumption; (4) obesity; and (5) attentional problems that adversely affect school performance. It then called for more and better (a) media education in schools; (b) scrutiny of media industry programming; (c) media education for pediatricians; and (d) pediatrician advice to parents on program selection, critical discussion of content with children, "limiting and focusing time spent with media," good parental role modeling, provision of alternative activities, media-free bedrooms, and avoidance of use of media as an electronic babysitter (p.342). Others may have explored the success of the first three recommendations, but there is no doubt that the fourth hit a nerve with the public.

Even so, there was no authoritative and widely-noticed mention of the notion of screen time until a couple of years later when, in 2001, the same committee published its report on media violence. With media violence then greatly in the public eye (as can be surmised from figure 6.1), this report urged that:

> Pediatricians should encourage parents to adhere to the AAP Media Education recommendations, including making thoughtful media choices and coviewing with children, limiting screen time (including television, videos, computer and

video games) to 1 to 2 hours per day, using the v-chip, avoiding violent video games in homes where they may be observed or played by young children, and keeping children's bedrooms media free. (p. 1224)

Although the AAP Media Education report does say that "Pediatricians should urge parents to avoid television viewing for children under the age of 2 years" (p.342), in fact, the 1–2 hour rule came from the much earlier report of the AAP's Committee on Communications on Children, Adolescents, and Television (1990). Concerned primarily about rising obesity among American children, and observing that "In 1989 the average child in the United States still spent more time watching television than performing any other activity except sleeping," this recommended that pediatricians advise parents to limit "television time" to 1–2 hours per day, following the advice of consultant Vic Strasburger (2018: 43).

And thus the famous (or perhaps infamous) 2x2 screen time rules were born. Thereafter, the term "screen time" is used increasingly often, by the AAP, the mass media and more widely in academic and policy discourses. At the time of writing, the AAP policy collection includes 74 statements on screen time, beginning in 2001 and linking use of television (mainly) to children's obesity, attention problems, smoking, violent behavior, and other problems.

It might be of regret or even frustration to the Academy that the press seemingly took little note of their other recommendations (on media education, for instance, or on the value of parent-child co-viewing). Instead, their guidance was translated for parents by journalists on the one hand, and clinicians, nurses, and other health professionals on the other, and they were transformed from guidance into hard-and-fast rules. Rules that seemed to apply irrespective of media content, or of a child's circumstances or needs. Rules that implied a dose-response relationship—so that for every hour (or quarter hour, even) that the limit was exceeded, the outcomes for the child would be worse; even though the research does not support such precision, and even though the adverse outcome itself was generally unspecified.

The Revision and Fall of Screen Time

The idea of screen time worked because it is simple, measurable, and memorable, needed by parents facing new technological uncertainties, and has science behind it. But it didn't work for similar reasons: its simplicity overrides the specifics of screen content and context; the focus on time measurement precludes attention to the quality of a child's engagement with the screen; it does not, in fact, help parents either in skilling their child for a digital future or building their resilience to technologically mediated harms.

Recognizing that children's media lives were changing, in 2016 the AAP revised its recommendations to offer families greater flexibility (Council on Communications and Media, 2016). The ban on screen time for infants and toddlers was brought down to those under 18 months old, and an exception made for interactive video chats. From 18 months, high-quality television content is acceptable, provided a parent watches with the child. For 2- to 5-year-olds, screen time should be limited to one hour per day, again, with parents present to help to interpret the content.

For older children, families are urged develop a "media plan" (the AAP provides an interactive tool), including designated "media-free" times. And parents are repositioned from policing screen time to acting as their child's "media mentor," including managing their own screen time as a model for their child. This last goes some way toward recognizing that, in the digital age, parents themselves have a measure of digital interests and expertise, and this could support their parenting and be of value to their child.

Although this revision was based on a new review of the scientific literature, one that recognized some positive as well as negative effects of screen time (Chassiakos et al., 2016), the evidence base has weaknesses. Most studies report correlations that are unable to substantiate the causal claim that increased screen time results in increased harm to children. Still, most of the research comes from the heyday of television rather than addressing today's digital and multimedia environment, especially its interactive forms. The evidence to support a one-hour limit for 2–5 year olds is hard to find, and only one study is cited on the benefits of Skype interactions for 18 month olds.

More importantly, the 2016 revision was too little, too late. For families, the idea of counting screen time as an indicator of likely harm has become increasingly problematic. For parents whose child plays several hours of sport and then likes to collapse in front of a screen, the idea that such viewing will cause obesity seems misplaced. For parents whose toddlers love to play in front of a noisy screen even though they're hardly looking at it, counting hours will surely raise unnecessary anxieties. For parents whose children are learning coding or creating their own video content or turning to YouTube to learn a new guitar chord, the lack of specificity about "screen use" is undermining. The rationale for a media plan, meanwhile, is sensible, and carefully argued, but it risks seeming to be middle-class proselytizing.

The most striking feature of figure 6.1 comes in the most recent period when, far from falling, attention to screen time sharply rises. Perhaps this was due to Twenge's (2017) book positioning the iPhone as the latest new technology to raise questions about screen time harms and children's welfare. Certainly her September 2017 article in *The Atlantic* entitled "Have smartphones destroyed a generation?" gathered worldwide attention. But it generated considerable criticism too, for rehashing the moral panics already addressed in the long history of previously "new" media, for inferring causation from correlation, neglecting to examine a range of more likely causes of childhood ills, and for over-interpreting descriptive statistics (Livingstone, 2018; Orben & Przybylski, 2019).

Indeed, recent years have been equally notable for a series of high profile reviews of the field drawing very modest conclusions regarding the importance of screen time. The World Health Organization's (2019) *Guidelines on physical activity, sedentary behaviour and sleep for children under 5 years of age* found little convincing evidence that screen time *per se* was the problem. In the UK, the Royal College of Paediatrics and Child Health published a systematic review of reviews which concluded that "the contribution of screen time to wellbeing is small when considered together with the contribution of sleep, physical activity, eating and bullying as well as poverty" (p.3). In the US, Odgers and Jensen (2020: 336) concluded from their recent review that:

> The most recent and rigorous large-scale preregistered studies report small associations between the amount of daily digital technology usage and adolescents' well-being that do not offer a way of distinguishing cause from effect and, as estimated, are unlikely to be of clinical or practical significance.

So the apparent recent peak in interest in screen time may evidence not its rise but its fall. In practical terms, this process has been unexpectedly accelerated by the COVID-19 pandemic of 2019–2021, for suddenly children globally, and especially in the United States and other wealthy countries where Internet access is widespread, have found themselves relying on screen media for their learning, information, communication, and entertainment. But in terms of policy and parenting advice, the controversy is revived—two hours a day of screen time may seem today like a quaint limit, but whether the result is good or bad for kids—this debate will, it seems, run and run:

Social Media Study Reveals Parents Ignore Screen Time Limits during COVID-19 (*Forbes*, 5/28/20).

Coronavirus Lockdowns Are Worsening Child Obesity due to Kids Spending an extra FIVE HOURS Per Day in Front of a Screen (*The Daily Mail*, 6/4/20)

Children's Daily Screen Time Skyrockets under Coronavirus Lockdown, and That's Not Necessarily a Bad Thing (*The Oregonian*, 5/28/20)

Toward a Solution

Wartella and Robb (2008: 8) argue that "not only is children's use of time of concern to parents, it is also public policy concern," and has been "at the root of the recurring controversies about children and media" over the past century, because "how children and adolescents spent their time became a barometer of their health and welfare during this period." But, after a huge scientific and policy effort, it is still not clear what kind of a barometer time use is, or what it tells us. However, from this effort, several points have become clear, and perhaps these show the way forward for those advising families on their children's media engagement, and for families themselves.

First, to paraphrase Schramm et al., no informed person can say simply that screen time is bad or good for children. Public anxieties always have and doubts always will arise as society innovates and embraces technological change. While public debate is too often panicky, extreme in its claims and often prejudiced in castigating those who use the technology "too much" or somehow "badly," the scientific attention and debate thereby attracted allows us to understand better the changes we are living through, and to reach some balanced recommendations.

Second, while parents talk about screen time rules with anxiety and guilt, at the same time their actions show how, in diverse and context-appropriate ways, they actively seek to engage with technological change in ways that are meaningful to them. What matters surely is to encourage families to gain needed skills, deliberate together on their values, and find a way of living in today's digital world, and bringing up their children, that suits their circumstances and interests.

Third, it is important to recognize that, salient though they are, digital technologies are but one of a long list of influences on children's welfare and life chances. Many other factors have repeatedly been shown to matter more. Some of these are under parents' control, more or less. Many of them are not, especially forms of socio-economic deprivation and other structural disadvantages that families face. To really make a difference to children's lives, therefore, we need to worry less about the child in front of the screen and pan back to see the bigger picture.

Notes

1. All italics from Schramm et al. are in the original.
2. The Merriam-Webster dictionary traces the first use of 'screen time' in this sense to 1921.
3. *The Guardian* claims that this is the first mention of screen time in its current use, but clearly the Hartford Courant long preceded this. https://www.theguardian.com/bo oks/2019/feb/01/from-cinema-to-smartphones-how-screen-time-became-a-problem
4. Notably, reports by the Annenberg Public Policy Center (1999) and the first UCLA Internet Report (2000).

References

Alper, M. (2014). *Digital youth with disabilities.* Cambridge, MA: MIT Press. https:// mitpress.mit.edu/books/digital-youth-disabilities

American Academy of Pediatrics. (1990). Committee on communications: Children, adolescents, and television. *Pediatrics,* 85(6), 1119–1120.

American Academy of Pediatrics. (1999). Committee on public education: Media education. *Pediatrics,* 104, 341–343.

American Academy of Pediatrics. (2001). Committee on public education: Media violence. *Pediatrics,* 108, 1222–1226.

Butsch, R. (2000). *The making of American audiences: From stage to television 1750–1990.* Cambridge, MA: Cambridge University Press.

Cairns, G., Angus, K., Hastings, G., & World Health Organization. (2009). *The extent, nature and effects of food promotion to children: A review of the evidence to December 2008.* World Health Organization. https://apps.who.int/iris/handle/10665/44237

Chassiakos, Y. L. R., Radesky, J., Christakis, D., Moreno, M. A., & Cross, C. (2016). Children and adolescents and digital media. *Pediatrics,* 138(5). doi: 10.1542/ peds.2016-2593

Council on Communications and Media. (2016). Media and young minds. *Pediatrics,* 138(5), e20162591–e20162591. doi: 10.1542/peds.2016-2591

Critcher, C. (2008). Making waves: Historic aspects of public debates about children and mass media. In K. Drotner & S. Livingstone (Eds.), *International handbook of children, media and culture* (pp. 91–104). London: SAGE.

Dorr, A. (1986). *Television and children: A special medium for a special audience.* Beverley Hills, CA: SAGE.

Himmelweit, H. T., Oppenheim, A. N., & Vince, P. (1958). *Television and the child: An empirical study of the effect of television on the young.* London: Nuffield Foundation and Oxford University Press.

Lee, E., Bristow, J., Faircloth, C., & Macvarish, J. (2014). *Parenting culture studies.* London: Palgrave Macmillan.

Livingstone, S. (2018). iGen: Why today's super-connected kids are growing up less rebellious, more tolerant, less happy—And completely unprepared for adulthood. *Journal of Children and Media,* 12(8), 118–123. doi: 10.1080/17482798.2017.1417091

Livingstone, S., & Blum-Ross, A. (2020). *Parenting for a digital future: How hopes and fears about technology shape children's lives.* New York: Oxford University Press.

Odgers, C. L., & Jensen, M. R. (2020). Annual research review: Adolescent mental health in the digital age: Facts, fears, and future directions. *Journal of Child Psychology and Psychiatry,* 61, 336–348. doi: 10.1111/jcpp.13190

Orben, A., & Przybylski, A. K. (2019). The association between adolescent well-being and digital technology use. *Nature Human Behavior,* 3, 173–182. doi: 10.1038/s41562-018-0506-1

Schramm, W., Lyle, J., & Parker, E. B. (1961). *Television in the lives of our children.* Stanford, CA: Stanford University Press.

Stiglic, N., & Viner, R. M. (2019). Effects of screentime on the health and well-being of children and adolescents: A systematic review of reviews. *BMJ Open,* 9(1), 1–15. doi: 10.1136/bmjopen-2018-023191

Strasburger, V. (2018). *The death of childhood.* New York: St Martin's Press.

Takeuchi, L., & Stevens, R. (2011). *The new coviewing: Designing for learning through joint media engagement.* New York: Joan Ganz Cooney Center.

Twenge, J. (2017). *iGen: Why today's super-connected kids are growing up less rebellious, more tolerant, less happy—And completely unprepared for adulthood.* New York: Atria Books.

Wartella, E., & Robb, M. (2009). Historical and recurring concerns about children's use of the mass media. In S. L. Calvert & B. J. Wilson (Eds.), *The handbook of children, media, and development* (pp. 5–26). Oxford: Blackwell. doi: 10.1002/9781444302752.ch1

World Health Organization. (2019). *Guidelines on physical activity, sedentary behaviour and sleep for children under 5 years of age.* World Health Organization. https://apps.who.int/iris/handle/10665/311664

Zaman, B., Holloway, D., Green, L., Jaunzems, K., & Vanwynsberghe, H. (2020). Opposing narratives about children's digital media use: A critical discourse analysis of online public advice given to parents in Australia and Belgium. *Media International Australia.* doi: 10.1177/1329878X20916950

CHAPTER 7

~

Why the Desensitization Effect Matters Most

Jeanne Funk Brockmyer

Introduction

This chapter examines the controversy about whether or not exposure to media violence has a harmful effect, in particular, a desensitization effect. The chapter emphasizes newer media (violent video games) and effects on children. First, desensitization is defined and the central role of empathy is explored. Next, research documenting desensitization effects from violent video game play is presented. Finally, the possible consequences of desensitization to violence are discussed and mitigation strategies are recommended.

Desensitization Defined

Recall a recent major tragedy. Possibly it was a school shooting. Now remember the first time you heard about a school shooting. Most likely the two reactions were very different because repeated exposure to the same traumatic event typically results in a decreased reaction. In 2018, CNN reported that there have been 288 school shootings since 2009 (https://www.cnn.com/2018/05/21/us/school-shooting-us-versus-world-trnd/index.html), and there have been many more since then. It is not surprising, therefore, that most people now have a decreased reaction to yet another school shooting, an example of desensitization to violence.

By definition, desensitization is the reduction or absence of a response to an event that would normally trigger a reaction (Brockmyer, 2015). Desensitization is typically an automatic, unconscious process that occurs gradually over several exposures to the desensitizing event. Desensitization affects what you think, how you feel, and how you react to a situation.

It is important to acknowledge that desensitization can be a normal reaction with a protective function. Imagine if you continued to have your initial reaction to every school shooting in the United States. Repetitively experiencing very strong feelings of horror and grief could be incapacitating. Desensitization can also be manipulated by a therapist, for example, to address unrealistic or exaggerated fear reactions. In that case, desensitization is a planned and desired outcome.

So why should there be any concern about desensitization to violence? The answer lies in the consequences. For example, although desensitization to the violence of school shootings has a protective function for individuals, it has probably also contributed to the failure of our society to find effective ways to prevent further shootings. In communities with high levels of real-life violence, desensitization to violence has been shown to lead to stronger proviolence attitudes, in other words, more acceptance of violence. People who are desensitized to violence are less likely to help a victim of violence. These are only a few examples of how desensitization to violence has negative consequences in the real world. In this chapter, violent video games are discussed as a potential cause of desensitization to real world violence due to alterations in empathy and moral reasoning.

Media Violence in the 2020s

The daily life of many American children is saturated with media. In 2010 it was estimated that the average 8 through 18-year-old in the United States spent more than 7 hours involved with media every day (Rideout et al., 2010). Today the Internet is overloaded with statistics about how children of various ages use the array of forms of media on their multiple platforms.

The fact that many contemporary media are violence-saturated has raised concern for parents, teachers, and professionals in many fields. Exposure to media violence, whether the realistic violence of news coverage, the lyrics of some popular music, the interactive violence of video games, or violent scenes in television or movies is essentially unavoidable. However, despite decades of research, the potential for negative effects following repeated exposure to media violence remains controversial. Most consumers of media violence, especially children and youth, do not believe they are adversely affected by media violence. There is even a handful of media researchers who deny such effects.

Others in this volume will address media violence research in depth. A few comments are needed here to inform the discussion of media-induced desensitization to violence. Over nearly seven decades, thousands of studies have been done to examine possible effects of media violence, with an emphasis on screen violence. Most contemporary media violence researchers believe that the body of research is conclusive: exposure to media violence does increase the relative risk of negative behaviors including aggression (Anderson et al., 2016). Media violence exposure is not the only contributing factor, but it is an important, potentially modifiable risk factor.

The reason for this increased risk is complicated. For some, exposure to violent media leads to angry thoughts and feelings. For others there are changes in how one perceives the actions of others (called the hostile attribution bias, benign actions such as being bumped in a crowded hallway are misinterpreted as intentional). Others, particularly young children, may simply imitate viewed aggression. In addition to increased negative behavior, there may be decreased positive behavior, such as failing to help people in need (for example, turning away from a bully terrorizing another person). At least in part, this increased potential for aggression and failure to aid others who are being victimized, may represent a desensitization effect.

Video Games

Video games are one of the newer forms of media, and considered to be especially likely to affect behavior. While some media (such as television and movies) primarily involve passive consumption, video game play is active. The player must continually choose actions, and in the violent games that tend to be popular with older children and adolescents, winning requires choosing violent actions. This creates a powerfully reinforcing situation: choose a violent action, then get rewarded with winning (and more points or other in-game rewards, and moving to a more advanced game level), and on and on.

In typical violent games, choosing the violent actions does not have any negative consequences. Often the violent actions are justified, and the consequences of violent actions are obscured. Several researchers have noted that violent video games are very effective teaching machines. Unfortunately, what is learned is that violence is fun, warranted and without negative consequences. For some individuals, this could lead to being desensitized to real-life violence. Desensitization to violence short-circuits empathic responding and blocks typical moral reasoning processes.

Empathy

Most would agree that empathy is a positive quality that is important to society. It is more difficult to agree on a specific definition of empathy, at least in part because it is studied by several different disciplines that do not always communicate with each other. There is agreement that empathy is best understood in terms of two components: emotional empathy and cognitive empathy. Emotional empathy is the sharing of the feelings of another, actually experiencing those feelings as if they are one's own feelings. Cognitive empathy is the understanding of another's feelings. Cognitive empathy has also been defined as being the ability to take the perspective of another person.

The Development of Empathy

Individuals are born with the foundation for empathy: One baby crying in a newborn nursery tends to trigger crying in the others. The development of true empathy requires a certain sequence of life experiences: Young infants indicate their needs by crying and it is important that they experience reliable, warm, responsive parenting. Later in the first year of life, into the second, the development of more complexity in emotion, cognition and motor skills leads to the capacity to develop basic prosocial behavior. At this point it is critical to see empathy modeled.

Empathy and empathic responding are strengthened through direct teaching including conversations about the perspective and feelings of others, and reinforcement of empathic choices. For example, if a child's younger sibling trips and starts crying, the older child could ridicule, comfort, or ignore the sibling. A child who comforts will hopefully receive a positive response from a parent who observes the interaction. Ridiculing or ignoring should prompt the parent to remind the child about how the younger sibling feels, thereby reinforcing the importance of taking the perspective of the other. As the child develops, continuing interactions with parents and siblings and with peers will contribute to further empathic maturation, finally resulting in the achievement of mature empathy.

Gender Differences in Empathy

The question of gender differences in empathy is complicated and the scientific literature is somewhat mixed. Most people believe that females are more empathic than males, and self-report measures reliably find higher empathy in females. However, results using more objective experimental methods are less consistent.

Some interesting information comes from nonhuman species, particularly those social species whose young require extended care. In these species, females (and not males) demonstrate basic empathic skills that indicate sensitivity to the emotional states of the young (Christov-Moorea et al.,

2014). Psychophysiological (this term refers to the physical foundation of psychological processes) research on the neural basis of empathy in humans suggests that the basic networks involved in emotional empathy are more developed in females. Such studies of human neural functioning, as well as animal research, are beginning to offer converging evidence that females do have the edge over males in empathy. This empathy advantage has hereditary roots in biology and is not either simply a result of social learning or an error related to research methods.

Moral Reasoning

In the earliest phases of development, a child's behavior is regulated by parents and other caregivers. As socialization progresses and moral standards are internalized, the capacity for moral reasoning develops and the child becomes able to distinguish between right and wrong. Moral reasoning is a psychological process that guides behavioral choice.

Moral reasoning undergoes developmental transformations throughout the life span. For example, preschoolers are most likely to reason simplistically, in ways that primarily benefit themselves. At elementary school age, moral reasoning starts to reflect concern for peer and adult approval, but children still tend to judge situations in simplistic "good" and "bad" terms. In adolescence, mature moral reasoning emerges, including abstract concerns about justice and caring for others. Adolescents gradually shift from external (typically defined by parents) to internalized behavioral regulation, taking responsibility for their own decisions and behaviors. When fully mature, moral reasoning includes behavioral self-monitoring: evaluating behavior in the context of personal moral standards and situational factors, and regulating actions by self-determined consequences. When personal moral standards are violated, this results in self-reproach and distress.

Mature empathy is necessary for the internalization and activation of moral reasoning. As mature empathy develops, it becomes an important prompt for the moral reasoning process and thus an important motivator for prosocial behavior. Feeling empathy alerts an individual to the moral relevance of a situation and triggers moral reasoning processes that aid in choosing a behavioral response.

Moral Disengagement

In a situation where someone is in need, typically an empathic response will trigger the moral reasoning process, leading to a prosocial response. If empathy is not triggered, moral reasoning will not be activated and moral disengagement may occur. Moral disengagement is a psychological process that occurs when moral standards are separated from actions. This allows the individual to engage in immoral behavior without feeling distress. Signs of moral disengagement include blaming immoral behavior on situational factors, misperceiving the significance and consequences of actions, and dehumanizing or blaming victims of immoral actions.

As a result of moral disengagement, immoral actions become acceptable to the individual and they do not experience the negative emotions that would typically result from behavior that is not consistent with internalized moral standards. A tendency for moral disengagement is a powerful predictor of several antisocial behaviors, including childhood aggression (Gini et al., 2014). Moral disengagement is a sign of impaired moral reasoning and may indicate desensitization.

Researchers have suggested that moral disengagement may explain why players enjoy playing violent video games. Violent video games typically have many cues that promote automatic moral disengagement including violence that is justified, dehumanization of characters, and distorted portrayal of consequences (Hartmann & Vorderer, 2010). If moral disengagement is not successful, then moral rationalization kicks in, most likely by thinking "it is just a game." With these mechanisms in place, virtual violence simply does not feel wrong, and since violent actions are justified, video game play can be guilt-free. However, when violence is not justified, research indicates that players do feel guilty, most likely because unjustified violence leads to an empathic response for victims, empathy triggers moral reasoning, and moral disengagement does not occur.

Research on Violent Video Game Effects

In this section research on desensitization to violence from violent video games will be briefly sampled, beginning with behavioral research, then proceeding to psychophysiological studies.

Behavioral Research

Researchers have been examining the effects of violent video games on aggression for over 30 years using several different research approaches. When enough research has been done with different research approaches, a meta-analysis can be done to summarize the findings and identify important trends across studies. A meta-analysis combines research on the same topic using very specific methodological and statistical procedures. Any deviation from the standard procedures can lead to an inaccurate conclusion.

Several meta-analyses, including two recent ones, have concluded that playing violent video games increases the relative risk of aggression (Mathur & VanderWeele, 2019; Prescott et al., 2018). Mathur and VanderWeele's meta-analysis examined three prior meta-analyses, two that agreed with the majority of research, and one that did not. Mathur and VanderWeele reported that there were procedural explanations for the different outcome of the diverging meta-analysis. Their final conclusion was that "… these conflicting meta-analyses in fact provide considerable consensus in favor of consistent, but small, detrimental effects of violent video games on aggressive behavior" (p. 707).

The research is now even more convincing: Playing violent video games increases the risk for aggressive behavior. However, the reason for this increase is still being examined. Desensitization to violence is one likely contributing factor. In a classic study, undergraduates played either a violent or a nonviolent video game, then were asked to complete a questionnaire while the researcher was out of the room. During questionnaire completion, a presumably real (but recorded) fight that resulted in injury was heard from behind a closed door, outside in the hallway. The experimenters timed how long it took the participant to offer help or, if no help was offered to the presumed victim, they asked whether the participant noticed the fight, and if they did notice it, to rate the severity of the fight.

Violent game players were less likely to try to offer help, more likely to delay offering help, less likely to notice the fight, and they judged the fight as less severe than the nonviolent game players. The researchers concluded that playing a violent video game desensitized players to the apparently real violence and, as a result, prevented helping (Bushman & Anderson, 2010). Similar research with children found the same effect. It seems likely that empathy was not triggered in those who played violent video games, and therefore the moral reasoning process was not engaged, leading to failure or delay in helping. This is an example of how desensitization to violence has a very negative effect that is not direct aggression.

Grizzard and colleagues examined desensitization by measuring guilt over five sessions of violent video game play. Players took the role of either a United Nations soldier or a terrorist on alternating days for four days of play. On the last day all participants played a different violent game as a terrorist. After playing, participants completed measures of guilt about actions they performed during game play. The researchers found that repeated exposure to the violent game decreased the first violent game's ability to cause guilt over the four-day period. This decrease in guilt about using violent actions in a game generalized to the second game even though it was only played once, suggesting that players had been desensitized to the violence (Grizzard et al., 2017).

Other researchers are examining moral disengagement. For example, Gabbiadini and colleagues examined pre-existing tendency for moral disengagement, as well as self-control, cheating, and aggression after high school students played either a violent or nonviolent video game. Exposure to violent video games was associated with lower self-control, more cheating, and more aggression (as measured by a laboratory task often used as a stand-in measure of aggression). This effect was most noticeable in people higher in pre-existing moral disengagement tendencies. This research suggests that, not only does playing violent video game create moral disengagement, but being more morally disengaged before playing can increase the effects of playing violent video games (Gabbiadini et al., 2014).

Yao and colleagues surveyed a large group of undergraduates who completed questionnaires measuring violent video game exposure, moral disengagement, aggressive tendencies, and sensation-seeking. A statistical analysis indicated that, similar to the findings of Gabbiandini and colleagues, college students with high levels of violent video game play were also higher in moral disengagement and aggressive tendencies (Yao et al., 2019). Desensitization to violence as a result of high exposure to violent video games likely played a role.

Psychophysiological Research

Studies documenting changes in physiological responses as a result of violent video game play are becoming a popular way to examine violent video game effects. One way to examine desensitization is to look for physiological changes in the level of arousal when individuals are exposed to a negative stimulus after playing violent video games. Arousal can be measured by examining changes in hormones such as cortisol, by studying changes in heart rate, or by looking directly at brain function. If the changes are less than expected, desensitization may have occurred. This section will describe a sample of representative research.

Some researchers have used electroencephalograms (EEG) to examine differences or changes in brain activity. The event-related potential (ERP) is a commonly used EEG-derived measure. An ERP is a brain response that is the direct result of a specific stimulus. Englehardt and colleagues used ERP to examine violent video game effects with young adults. These participants reported their history of violent video game play, played either a violent or nonviolent video game, and viewed violent and nonviolent photos while having brain activity measured.

Comparing participants low in prior exposure only, those who played a violent game had a lower response in a component of the ERP to the violent photos, compared with those who played a nonviolent game. This suggests that playing the violent game desensitized the low exposure players to violence in the photos. Compared to low-exposure participants, high-exposure participants had a lower ERP response to violent images, suggesting long-term desensitization (Englehardt et al., 2011).

Several researchers have used functional magnetic resonance imaging (fMRI) to study the effects of violent video game play on individual brain function. fMRI measures brain activity by demonstrating changes associated with blood flow. These changes demonstrate neural activation because when an area of the brain is being used, blood flow to that area increases. Findings on violent video game effects have been somewhat inconsistent, depending on what area of the brain is being examined, specific participant characteristics, and actions possible in the violent video game.

Gentile and colleagues studied 13 young adults who reported a history of either violent or nonviolent gaming. The participants then played a video game in both a violent and nonviolent mode while undergoing fMRI scanning. Participants with predominantly nonviolent gaming experience had an increase in activation of emotional response regions when playing the violent game, while violent gamers demonstrated an active suppression of emotional response regions. The authors suggest that those with a history of predominantly violent game play are demonstrating a desensitization effect due to their long-term exposure to violent video games (Gentile et al., 2016).

In contrast, Szycik and colleagues used digital pictures showing painful or non-painful everyday situations (for example a hand cut by a knife) to study the fMRI responses of 40 young adult males who had either low or high prior violent video game experience. They found no difference in the neural correlates of empathy, suggesting no desensitization effect from long-term violent video game exposure (Szycik et al., 2017). However, the images in this study may not have been extreme enough to elicit a measurable difference in empathic response.

The fact that results of fMRI studies of desensitization from exposure to violent video games are mixed is not surprising. Compared with behavioral research, psychophysiological research is in its infancy. In addition to short-term studies, long-term research is needed to fully understand this issue. Overall, the current body of both behavioral and psychophysiological research does suggest that desensitization to violence can be a result of exposure to violent video games.

Addressing the Problem of Violent Video Games and Desensitization to Violence

The desensitization effect of exposure to violent video games is a public health issue. However, it does not appear that legislation is a way to regulate access to violent games. Even modest attempts to regulate violent video games such as enforcing age-based ratings and prohibiting sale to children under the rated age have been successfully challenged, all the way to the Supreme Court. In 2011 the Supreme Court upheld lower courts' opinions that the state of California could not ban the sale of violent video games to children younger than the age rating (the penalty was to be a $1,000 fine to the retailer who sold the game). The majority of the Supreme Court viewed violent video games as an art form protected by the First Amendment despite the fact that there are forms of speech, such as obscenity, that are considered to be beyond such protection.

Parents are the key to preventing and mitigating the impact of desensitization to violence triggered by playing violent video games. Parents need to be aware of the content of the video games their children are playing. Game content is rated by the Entertainment Software Rating Board (ESRB, www.esrb.org). The ESRB system indicates the ages for which a game is appropriate. There are also thirty content descriptors, including six for violence (cartoon, fantasy, sexual, and intense violence as well as references to violent acts and violence with no descriptor). Interactive descriptors indicate whether users can interact with each other, share their location with other users, purchase digital goods or services, and if unrestricted Internet access is provided.

All ratings are displayed on physical game packages, on games that are downloaded, in advertisements, in social media and on websites where games are reviewed. The ESRB also has a phone application that can be downloaded for free from the website. The application can be used to look up rating information and read rating summaries for all games. Several researchers have questioned the adequacy of the ESRB ratings system and, although the current system has been improved from the original age-based only system, there is room for further development. Parents should use the age ratings only as loose guidance for what is appropriate for their child.

Most importantly, parents need to apply their own moral standards and their knowledge of their child's cognitive, social, and emotional level when deciding which games are appropriate. After considering descriptions of game content, parents should watch children play a video game through more than one level, as content changes as the game progresses. Playing the game is an even better way to be exposed to game content. Parents and children should have a conversation that examines the consequences of the unreal violence of video games compared with the real-life consequences of violence. Reasonable rules should be set about time spent playing any video games while considering other demands on the child's life and the need for creative play.

Parents should become familiar with recommendations of professional organizations such as the American Academy of Pediatrics. One of their publications may be especially useful: Video Games: Establish Your Own Family's Rating System (https://www.healthychildren.org/English/family-life/Media/Pages/Video-Games-Set-Your-Own-Ratings-System .aspx).

For parents who want to provide a constructive video game experience for their child there is a genre of video games called Serious Games. These games have a goal other than entertainment, but they engage players with a strong element of fun and reward. Some serious games are made to teach specific skills, while others teach values such as empathy. For more information about Serious Games for children, see https://www.seriousgames.net/home/playful-learning/

Schools also have a role to play in preventing and mitigating the effects of violent video games. Many primary schools have adopted various types of social emotional learning practices, including empathy training and emotion understanding. The guiding principle for such practices is that by developing positive behaviors early on, it should be possible to avoid the development of negative emotions and behavior. Social emotional learning practices also have a positive impact on academic performance.

One typical approach is for the teacher to read a story about a common life experience to the class. The class then discusses the emotions in the situation described, and then they relate these emotions to their personal life experiences. A meta-analysis examining the effect of such empathy training with children, adolescents, and adults found that, overall, empathy training increases levels of empathy (Tedding Van Berkhout & Malouff, 2015). Increasing an individual's capacity for empathy may be protective for the effects of desensitizing experiences such as exposure to violent video games, but long-term research is needed to confirm this effect.

A structured program to encourage positive behavior for grades pre-K through 12 can be purchased from the Positivity Project (posproject.org). The Positivity Project provides teacher training and a package of lessons, charts, and activities. Their philosophy is that it is critically important for children and adolescents to build positive relationships. In order to do that, it is necessary to build specific character strengths such as social intelligence, kindness, self-control, and curiosity.

Media literacy training is an intervention that targets developing critical thinking skills about media content. Research on media literacy's effectiveness has been done with a range of media, however studies specifically on mitigating the effects of violent video games are limited. The goal of media literacy for violent media is to change the child's attitudes about the realism and appropriateness of media violence. A three-session intervention designed to change adolescents' attitudes toward violence and their intention to play violent video games was successful with better-adjusted adolescents. However, for those adolescents with problematic lifestyles (such as drug use), intention to play violent video games actually increased (Rivera et al., 2016).

In summary, parents have the central role to play in first limiting children's exposure to violent video games, and then mitigating potential effects by engaging their children and adolescents in discussions of violent game content and violence in the real world. Preventive interventions in schools can strengthen empathy and reduce tendencies for desensitization to violence and moral disengagement. It is unclear how effective media literacy training about violent content will be with particularly vulnerable groups, especially adolescents with other risk factors.

Conclusion

The ultimate question is not simply whether research finds an effect of exposure to violent video games, but rather what the long-term implications are for everyday behavior. Consider a world where most individuals are desensitized to violence. Conflict of all kinds would likely increase, from children arguing and fighting on the playground, to an increase in child abuse and domestic violence, to a surge in international conflict. Helping would decrease. Adults would be slower to intervene in children's fights. Fewer would choose low-paying helping positions, for example, in social services, or high-risk jobs like firefighting and police work. Nations would turn their backs on conflict harming people in other countries. Charities would suffer.

Exposure to violent video games is a significant risk factor for desensitization to violence in susceptible children and youth. Desensitization to violence can disrupt empathy and moral reasoning and allow moral disengagement. Susceptible individuals may develop callous and cold personality characteristics that disrupt interpersonal relationships. Desensitization to violence is a gateway for aggressive behavior and a barrier to prosocial behavior. This makes desensitization to violence perhaps the most serious consequence of exposure to violent video games.

References

Anderson, C. A., Bushman, B. J., Bartholow, B. D., Cantor, J., Christakis, D., Coyne, S. M., Donnerstein, E., Brockmyer, J. F. Gentile, D. A., Green, C. S., Huesmann, R., Hummer, T., Krahe, B., Strasburger, V. C., Warburton, W., Wilson, B., J., & Ybarra, M. (2017). Screen violence and youth behavior. *Pediatrics, 140*(s2), S142–S147. doi: 10.1542/peds.2016-1758T

Brockmyer, J. F. (2015). Playing violent video games and desensitization to violence. *Child and Adolescent Psychiatric Clinics of North America, 24*, 65–77. doi: 10.1016/j.chc.2014.08.001

Bushman, B. J., & Anderson, C. A. (2009). Comfortably numb: Desensitizing effects of violent media on helping others. *Psychological Science, 20*(3), 273–277.

Christov-Moorea, L., Simpson, E. A., Coudéb, G., Grigaitea, K., Iacobonia, M., & Ferrarib, P. F. (2014).

Empathy: Gender effects in brain and behavior. *Neuroscience and Biobehavioral Reviews, 46*(Pt 4), 604–627. doi: 10.1016/j.neubiorev.2014.09.001

Englehardt, C. R., Bartholow, B. D., Kerr, G. T., & Bushman, B. J. (2011). This is your brain on violent video games: Neural desensitization to violence predicts increased aggression following violent video game exposure. *Journal of Experimental Social Psychology, 47*, 1033–1036. doi: 10.1016/j.jesp.2011.03.027

Gabbiadini, A., Riva, P., Andrighetto, L., Volpato, C., & Bushman, B. J. (2014). Interactive effect of moral disengagement and violent games on self-control, cheating and aggression. *Social Psychological and Personality Science, 5*(4), 451–458. doi: 10.1177/1948550613509286

Gentile, D. A., Swing, E. L., Anderson, C. A., Rinker, D., & Thomas, K. M. (2016). Differential neural recruitment during violent video game play in violent and non-violent players. *Psychology of Popular Media Culture, 5*(1), 39–51. doi: 10.1037/ppm0000009

Gini, G., Pozzoli, T., & Hymel, S. (2014). Moral disengagement among children and youth: A meta-analytic review of links to aggressive behavior. *Aggressive Behavior, 40*, 56–68. doi: 10.1002/ab.21502

Grizzard, M., Tamborini, R., Sherry, J., & Weber, R. (2017). Repeated play reduces video games' ability to elicit guilt: Evidence from a longitudinal experiment. *Media Psychology, 20*, 267–290. doi: 10.1080/15213269.2016.1142382

Hartmann, T., & Vorderer, P. (2010). It's okay to shoot a character: Moral disengagement in violent video games. *Journal of Communication, 60*, 94–119. doi: 10.1111/j.1460-2466.2009.01459.x

Mathur, M. B., & VanderWeele, T. J. (2019). Finding common ground in meta-analysis "wars" on violent video games. *Perspectives on Psychological Science, 14*, 705–708. doi: 10.1177/1745691619850104

Prescott, A. T., Sargent, J. D., & Hull, J. G. (2018). Metaanalysis of the relationship between violent video game play and physical aggression over time. *Proceedings of the National Academy of Sciences USA, 115*, 9882–9888.

R Development Core Team. www.pnas.org/cgi/doi/10.1073/pnas.1611617114

Rideout, V. J., Foehr, U. G., & Roberts, D. F. (2010). *Generation M2: Media in the lives of 8- to 18-year-olds*. Menlo Park, CA: Kaiser Family Foundation.

Rivera, R., Santos, D., Brändle, G., & Cärdaba, M. A. (2016). Design effectiveness analysis of a media literacy intervention to reduce violent video games consumption among adolescents: The relevance of lifestyles segmentation. *Evaluation Review, 40*(2), 142–161. doi: 10.1177/0193841X16666196

Szycik, G. R., Mohammadi, B., Münte, T. F., & te Wildt, B. T. (2017). Lack of evidence that neural empathic responses are blunted in excessive users of violent video games: An fMRI study. *Frontiers in Psychology, 8*(174). doi: 10.3389/fpsyg.2017.00174

Teding van Berkhout, E., & Malouff, J. M. (2016). The efficacy of empathy training: A meta-analysis of randomized controlled trials. *Journal of Counseling Psychology, 63*(1), 32–41. doi: 10.1037/cou0000093

Yao, M., Zhou, Y., Li, J., & Gao, X. (2019). Violent video games exposure and aggression: The role of moral disengagement, anger, hostility, and disinhibition. *Aggressive Behavior, 45*, 662–670. doi: 10.1002/ab.21860

~

About the Editor and Contributors

Editor

Victor C. Strasburger is a pediatrician and adolescent medicine specialist. He is the founding chief of the Division of Adolescent Medicine and Distinguished Professor of Pediatrics Emeritus at the University of New Mexico School of Medicine in Albuquerque, USA, where he has worked for the past 33 years. He has authored more than 200 articles and papers and 14 books (including one novel) on the subjects of adolescent medicine, and the effects of media on children and adolescents. He is the co-author of the American Academy of Pediatrics' famous two-hour media rule for children and adolescents and several other AAP policy statements. Dr Strasburger is a Fulbright Scholar who has lectured in 48 of the 50 United States and on 5 continents, and has appeared on "Oprah," the "Today" show, and NPR.

Contributors

El-Lim Kim is currently pursuing a PhD degree in social psychology at Iowa State University. She has obtained her master's degree in developmental psychology at Ewha Womans University. Her current research interest lies on the media effect. Specifically, she designed and carried out various research studies to investigate the impact of media on aggressive behaviors and sexual objectification of women.

Craig A. Anderson is Distinguished Professor of Psychology, Iowa State University. His early work focused on attribution theory and social judgment processes. His current work focuses on the General Aggression Model, a bio-social-cognitive model integrating aggression theories from social, personality, developmental, and cognitive psychology. Much of his recent empirical work involves media effects. In 2017, Dr. Anderson received the *Kurt Lewin Award* from the Society for the Psychological Study of Psychological Issues, for "outstanding contributions to the development and integration of psychological research and social action." In 2018, Dr. Anderson received the Society for Personality and Social Psychology's *Distinguished Scholar Award*. His 240plus publications have yielded over 50,000 citations, placing him in the top 3 media, violence, and aggression scholars.

Douglas A. Gentile is an award-winning research scientist, educator, author, and is Professor of Psychology at Iowa State University. He has authored well over 100 peer-reviewed scientific journal articles, including studies on the positive and negative effects of video games on children in several countries, how screen time contributes to youth obesity, and gaming disorder. A Fellow of the American Psychological Association, the Association for Psychological Science, the Society for Personality and Social Psychology, and the Society for the Psychological Study of Social Issues, he was also named one of the top 300 professors in the United States by the Princeton Review.

Wayne A. Warburton is an associate professor in developmental psychology at Macquarie University, Australia, and is also a registered psychologist. His research interests centre on aggressive behavior, violent and prosocial media, and screen addiction. He is co-author of several statements by international panels of experts on topics such as media violence and youth violence, including for the US Supreme Court. He has won more than 25 awards for his research, scholarship and teaching, most recently the 2018 Distinguished Scientific Contributions to Media Psychology and Technology Award from the American Psychological Association.

Paul J. Wright received his PhD at The University of Arizona with emphases in communication and family studies and human development. He is a full professor of communication science in The Media School at Indiana University, Bloomington. He is also the director of the Communication Science Unit, a core faculty partner at The Center for Sexual Health Promotion, and an affiliate faculty member with The Kinsey Institute. He was ranked by *Communication Education* as in the top 1% of communication and media research productivity worldwide.

Helena M. McAnally. Dr. McAnally has worked on a number of projects focussing on youth well-being and has also worked on Dunedin Study research focussing on the impact of television viewing in childhood and later mental health. She currently manages the Next Generation Study, which assesses the children of Dunedin Study members once those children have turned 15.

Robert J. Hancox, MD. Professor Hancox is a respiratory physician with varied research interests. He has been working with Dunedin Study data since 2002 and has led the investigation of the long-term effects of childhood television viewing in the study. He is also the principal investigator of the Next Generation Study.

Sonia Livingstone, OBE, is professor of social psychology in the Department of Media and Communications at LSE. Her research examines how the changing conditions of mediation are reshaping everyday practices and possibilities for action. She has published twenty books on media audiences, media literacy and media regulation, with a particular focus on the opportunities and risks of digital media use in the everyday lives of children and young people. She has advised the UK government, European Commission, European Parliament, Council of Europe and other national and international organizations on children's rights, risks and safety in the digital age. She was awarded the title of Officer of the Order of the British Empire (OBE) in 2014 "for services to children and child internet safety."

Jeanne Funk Brockmyer is Distinguished University Professor, Emerita, in the Department of Psychology, University of Toledo, Toledo, OH. A clinical psychologist, Dr. Brockmyer's research has focused on children and violence, particularly media violence, emphasizing possible effects on empathy and desensitization to violence. Brockmyer and her research colleagues have developed measures of empathy, attitudes toward violence, and game engagement that have been widely adopted in video game research.

www.ingramcontent.com/pod-product-compliance
Lightning Source LLC
Chambersburg PA
CBHW050534270326
41926CB00015B/3227

9 781475 855227